THE YEAR THROUGH
CHRISTIAN EYES

W. R. MATTHEWS, KCVO, DD
DEAN EMERITUS OF SAINT PAUL'S

THE YEAR
THROUGH
CHRISTIAN
EYES

LONDON
EPWORTH PRESS

Set in 12/13 pt Bembo
and printed and bound
in Great Britain by
W & J Mackay & Co Ltd
at their works in Fair Row
Chatham

SBN 7162 0133 X

Contents

Foreword

◇◇◇◇◇◇◇◇◇◇◇◇◇◇◇◇◇◇◇◇❋◇◇◇◇◇◇◇◇◇◇◇◇◇◇◇◇◇◇◇◇

More than thirty years ago, as a schoolboy with a pre-ternatural interest in religion, I was an avid listener to BBC services and talks. I would rush home from school to hear evensong from St Paul's Cathedral on Wednesdays and usually switch on 'the wireless' for broadcast worship before going with my father to our Methodist Chapel on Sunday mornings. How well I remember Sunday after-noon tea in our terraced house, my parents and myself seated at table in the living-room, with tinned fruit and my mother's currant cake and an ecclesiastical voice from the loudspeaker!

'They were giants in those days.' One recalls Anthony Deane on the New Testament, Bernard Clements, most homely and profound of spiritual teachers, Edward Woods, ecumenical bishop, Vincent McNabb, the Dominican, C. C. Martindale, the Jesuit (how we loved to applaud a Roman Catholic and recognize Methodist affinities!), and the great leaders, Cosmo Lang and William Temple.

Some, whom we knew well by voice, are still with us, J. S. Whale and Leslie Weatherhead are in retirement, though Donald Soper still maintains Christ's cause at Kingsway, the Lords, Hyde Park and on television. But the *doyen* is, appropriately, a Dean—W. R. Matthews, who resigned from St Pauls in 1967 after thirty-three years and who still preaches each Saturday by his pen in the *Daily Telegraph*. It has been one of the delights and privileges of the last few years to get to know this boyhood hero personally.

Well towards the end of his eighth decade, W. R. Matthews still has those qualities for which in his prime he was renowned, clarity of mind and expression, the ability to confront issues fully and honestly, an understanding of the spirit of the age and a gentle, reconciling temper. He has been a Christian thinker throughout the most bewildering period of man's history, which has not left his own life untouched by sorrow; yet his liberality has never failed. No harsh condemnation of change has issued from his lips or pen. He has seen evil and deplored it, but he has retained the mind of a Christian philosopher.

Dr Matthews could not be other than an Anglican and he belongs to that glorious tradition of his Church, of which his predecessor at St Pauls, W. R. Inge, was also a representative, the tradition of the Cambridge Platonists and of such nineteenth-century scholars as Milman, Mansell and Hort. This does not dethrone the intellect or make the dichotomy between reason and revelation too sharp, or split the personality into heart and mind; yet it is not coldly rational or dispassionate, it does not attempt to reduce experience to bloodless categories; it is not indeed reductionist at all except in its desire to make an end of excess, of cruelty, superstition, tyranny and evil. To a greater extent than Inge, has Matthews been hospitable to liberal Catholics as well as liberal evangelicals. He preached at the jubilee of All Saints, Margaret Street, in 1939. Yet there is a sentence from Inge, which may be applied to Matthews' spirituality: 'Sometimes the consciousness of communion with God is a calm and gentle feeling, compounded . . . of awe and love, a feeling which opens new vistas to the eye of the soul, but does not banish reason from her seat.'

I have used the fashionable term 'spirituality'. Dean Matthews once said jokingly to me, 'I hope I don't become a spiritual classic!' There is nothing precious or pietistic about his Christianity; it has more of the study than the cell.

These pieces are a selection from the *Daily Telegraph* articles during the 1960s. They belong to the central page of that great newspaper, along with the leaders and 'Peterborough', the correspondence columns and the special articles. They do not advocate 'a fugitive and cloistered virtue'. The events and circumstances of the world are no passing illusion. They are reality, but not the only or the ultimate reality. 'God was in Christ reconciling the world unto himself.' And so the Christian lives in two times at once—the time of the world and the time of the gospel. As he reads the news or engages in business or politics, he lives by faith in a Divine, ever-active grace, which includes yet transcends all things.

Dr Matthews' religion begins in thought—honest, rigorous, wrestling—and ends in prayer and the worship of the Church. As presented here, these articles should be both exercises in the application of Christian wisdom to the world, and religious meditations.

In his time, the Dean has composed prayers. One of them, which has been set to music by Walker Robson and sung as a choir anthem, may fittingly introduce this volume. With an echo—conscious or unconscious—of Newman, it is at once Anglican, evangelical, and Catholic and enshrines the adamantine faith which has undergirded W. R. Matthews' prolific writings and long life:

Thou hast a work for me to do; O Lord, show it to me: Thou hast a place for me to fill; give me grace to fill it to Thy glory: Thou hast given me a soul to make; make Thou it for me, and build me into Thy spiritual temple, for Jesus' sake.

GORDON S. WAKEFIELD

The Author and Publishers are grateful to the *Daily Telegraph*, in which these pieces first appeared, and to Mr G. A. Moynihan of the Epworth Press for help in their selection and preparation.

First Sunday in Advent

BY LOVE OR FEAR

The hymns of the Church for the Advent season are among the most moving and thrilling in the whole corpus of Christian hymnody. 'Lo! He comes, with clouds descending, once for favoured sinners slain'—the verses ring like a trumpet still, even in the sophisticated ears of men conditioned by modern scientific culture.

One reason for their power over our imaginations is that they appeal to some profound emotions, they express exultation, loving expectancy—and dread. In the New Testament exultation and loving expectancy are uppermost; they breathe in the simple words which conclude the last book in the Bible, 'Amen, Lord Jesus, come'.

In later times, however, by a significant historical irony the predominant feeling about the Second Coming appears to have been panic fear. From time to time men have arisen who persuaded multitudes that they knew the date of the end of the world; the result has been widespread terror followed by a sigh of relief when the date was safely passed. The heart-felt prayer has been, 'Don't come, Lord Jesus'.

'Save, Lord, by love or fear', runs a line of a well-known hymn, and we must own that dread, or awe, has a necessary place in any religious experience which is not merely sentimentality. Perhaps, too, the fear of God and His judgement is often the starting point of the process of salvation, but the consummation of the process cannot be reached under the impulse of fear, for we do not begin to know God until we turn to Him with love and at least conceive the possibility that our impulse of love is in truth, a response to His love for us.

In all our reflections on the judgement we must hold fast to the fundamental Christian belief that God is love and, therefore, that any doctrine which really contradicts this must be false. It follows from this that when we think of the divine judgement we must always think of it as the judgement of love.

This does not mean that it ceases to be judgement, or that we can regard it with light-hearted confidence. In some respects the judgement of love can be more shattering than the judgement of impersonal authority. Many a sinner, who faced a court and public opinion with comparative indifference, has been pierced to the heart by the thought of the agony of some one person who loved him and, while judging him, loves him still. This judgement of love can have a healing and restoring virtue which impersonal justice cannot have.

Among all the Christian heresies that of Origen attracts me—if it is a heresy. That early Christian thinker held that the infinitely patient love of God would, in the end, be triumphant in every soul. The rebellious spirit, he believed, would be led through many states of existence in which the love of God both judged him and wooed him, until at last all were brought home to the Father's house.

Before we reject this opinion let us remember that Jesus compared the seeking love of God to a shepherd looking for a lost sheep and never giving up until he found it; and God does not change.

Second Sunday in Advent

When Cranmer composed the Collect for the second Sunday in Advent he had in mind the idea that men reading the Bible in good faith would find in it the simple gospel and the way of their own resolutions. The Scriptures were 'written for our learning' and now, when he wrote, were open free for all to hear and study. The expectation was not altogether realized, for differences of meaning seemed to multiply, but beyond doubt the quest for the simple gospel which all can understand and accept was an important element in the religion of our people. It is so still. How far may we expect it to succeed?

The Christian gospel can be presented at almost every level of human understanding. It can be presented as a wonderful story, and children who have been taught their religion 'at their mother's knee' are likely to remember it all their lives. That may be a very good thing, if they grow up to understand Tennyson's words, 'truth embodied in a tale'; it may be bad, if they never grow up. The story of God who loved the world so much that He gave His only Son to save it, and of the Son who suffered and rose from death to open the way for us to heaven, to live with Him always, is comprehensible to a child—perhaps more comprehensible than to adults. Anyone who has experience of the difficult art of story-telling to children will know that there is development in audience-response. At first the child likes to hear his favourite story over and over again, protesting vehemently against any change. There comes an evening when the words Why? and How? make their disturbing appearance. How did Cinderella's pumpkin change into a coach, and why were her slippers made of glass? The stage of criticism has come, and if the questions are not plausibly answered the story will be deleted from the nursery canon.

This happened with the simple gospel and the child hearer. If we have told the story well, the questions will come. Why did Jesus have to die for us? What do we need to be saved from? Does God punish Jesus for our sins? Where is Heaven? And so indefinitely. I have come across hard-headed businessmen who dismiss the New Testament as 'a collection of fairy tales'. They are probably men who, when they were children, had asked questions and been told to hold their tongues, or fobbed off by some evasion. The 'simple gospel' is the vehicle of profound, and indeed inexhaustible, truth, and only by asking questions do we progress in understanding. And of course one of the first questions can only be answered day by day; it is the practical question arising out of the simple gospel, 'Lord, what must I do?'

Third Sunday in Advent

QUIET MINISTRIES

When, in the Collect for the third Sunday in Advent, we pray for 'the ministers and stewards of Christ's mysteries' we are doubtless intended to think first of all of ordained ministers; but not only of them, for we must not forget 'the priesthood of the laity' on which the New Testament insists. The work of the ministry is the concern and responsibility of the whole Church and of every member of it. An instructive exercise would be to read through the Epistles noting the names of men and women who are mentioned as 'helps'. Of a few we have some slight information, but, for the most part, we know only their names, and there must have been many others who have no record. It is good to remember these people who have remained obscure, as they were in their life-time, but who took a vital part in the beginning of the Christian Church—ordinary, quiet persons who were truly 'ministers'.

We may trace them back into the Gospels, for it is clear that our Lord had friends and helpers who were not Apostles. According to St Matthew, there were a number of women watching the Crucifixion from a distance who had followed Jesus from Galilee and we are told who three of them were. They stayed, it seems, when the Apostles had run away. Joseph of Arimathaea, who buried the body of the Lord, was evidently one of the quiet ministers of the Kingdom of God.

Christians are rightly urged to contribute towards the recruitment and training of men who have a vocation to the ordained ministry of the Church, but when we have sent our cheque our duty is not finished. We know how St Paul and the other Apostles depended on the co-operation and prayers of the members of their churches; do we suppose that men who in the twentieth century strive to carry on the work of the Apostles can do without them?

One of the causes of the rapid spread of Christianity in the first century was the fact that everyone who was baptized was made fully aware that he had a ministry of witness. Wherever he was and whatever his occupation he must commend the gospel of Christ and be ready to 'give a reason for the hope that was in him'. I do not imagine that many of them launched out into oratory or spoke at street corners, for they were mostly quiet and humble individuals; they witnessed in their conversation and their lives, showing forth 'the wisdom of the just'.

Many of us probably would confess that they owe much to some layman who was one of these quiet ministers. Perhaps he was not learned and could not argue about theology, but the spirit of Christ shone upon us through him. Of such persons let us think with gratitude and pray that we too may have some share in this ministry.

Fourth Sunday in Advent

◇◇◇◇◇◇◇◇◇◇◇◇◇◇◇◇◇◇◇◇✳◇◇◇◇◇◇◇◇◇◇◇◇◇◇◇◇◇◇◇◇

PREPARE FOR JOY

Throughout the land in almost every home preparations for Christmas joy are going forward; the presents are being planned and the materials for the feast assembled. All but the very foolish understand that these things are not enough and that joy has a spiritual fount; all the good things will be of no avail without a merry heart.

The Christian is acquainted with joy. St Paul, in today's Epistle (Philippians 4:4–7), writes 'Rejoice in the Lord always, and again I say rejoice.' Every day of our lives we should have joy. But few of us could say that this is our experience; 'rarely comest thou spirit of delight' would express our religion. Christmas is one of the days when we must try to recapture joy.

But we cannot hope to do this without preparation any more than we could expect to provide a Christmas dinner on the spur of the moment. We must prepare, of course, by fixing our attention and our aspiration on the coming of Christ and all that it means to our souls and to the world. This is obvious, but do we see clearly enough that, along with this, we have to eliminate certain things which are the enemies of joy? Let us think of some of them.

Often we shall find that the chief obstacle to joy is a sin of which we have not repented. It may indeed be one of which we are not fully aware, a sin which is partly secret even to us. But though we may have almost repressed it and banished it from memory, it is nagging at us below the surface of consciousness. We shall never know free and unclouded joy until we have brought it out into the light, seen it for what it is, repented of it and been forgiven.

'Never be glad except when thou canst look on the face of thy brother in love', so runs an alleged saying of Jesus which does not appear in the New Testament. Genuine or not, it breathes the spirit of our Master. It is a signpost to joy. For when we are not thinking about our grievances we know very well that all such emotions as hatred, envy, contempt and jealousy are sources of vexation and even of mental torture; we know too that rejoicing over our enemies is a bastard and delusive joy. When we prepare for joy let us clear our hearts of every vestige of ill will. Perhaps, by the grace of God, we may pass from the negative to the positive and begin to love our enemies.

On Christmas day we shall rejoice in the company of our families and friends—a dear and narrow circle. To spare a thought for those who are outside and have no cheer or warmth of loved companionship will enhance our joy if we do not rest content with thinking but do something, sacrifice something, to ease their loneliness and brighten their lot.

In this troublesome world thoughtful men cannot banish *Weltschmerz* even on Christmas day, and we ought to reflect upon the needs and dangers of mankind, but never in a mood of hopelessness or despair. Though, to a large extent, the world has forgotten Him, God has not forgotten the world. The joy of Christmas day springs from the faith that 'God so loved the world that He gave His only begotten Son'. He loves it still and works unceasingly for its redemption.

Christmas Day

THE SON AND THE WORD

A Christmas Meditation on the divine adventure of the Creation and redemption of the world

In the Epistle and Gospel for Christmas Day we hear our wonderful English version at its greatest. In the first, the majestic rhythms of the opening verses of the Epistle to the Hebrews attune us to solemnity; in the second, the Prologue to St John's Gospel, we are moved by the simplicity of the pregnant statements.

In each there is a memorable sentence which stays in our mind like a haunting tune: 'God hath in these last days spoken unto us by his Son' (Hebrews 1:2), and 'The Word was made flesh, and dwelt among us, . . . full of grace and truth' (John 1:14).

These are indeed lovely words, but they have more than literary beauty; they are great words to express great thoughts, and they derive their power from the far-reaching truths which their writers were trying to convey. We have in the Christmas Epistle and Gospel, in fact, classical statements of the two principal metaphors, or symbols, which are employed in the New Testament to explain the meaning of the coming of Christ into the world and the significance of His personality. They are the answer to the question, What has He done for us? They are two guiding stars for all our thoughts on the Person and Work of Christ.

Yet they are two symbols and not one, and, at first sight, it may appear that they are very different from one another, for, after all, a word is quite unlike a son.

When we read these passages, however, we observe that their writers were far from thinking that they were contradictory; the Son could also be Word, and the Word the Son. The writer to the Hebrews represents Christ as the fulfilment and the culmination of the work of the Prophets. The word of God had been given to them, and they had proclaimed it as ministers, as servants, but now, at the end of the prophetic period, the Word of God has been spoken to us 'through his Son'.

St John sets out from the thought of the Word which 'was in the beginning with God and was God', but of 'the Word made flesh' he writes, 'we beheld his glory, the glory as of the only-begotten of the Father': The Word is also Son.

The history of Christian thought on the Incarnation does not stop with the New Testament. In one sense it begins there, for the New Testament forms the starting point, and the norm, of a long process of discussion and reflection.

It was inevitable that there should be attempts to draw out the meaning of the New Testament data and to answer questions which seemed to arise; perhaps, too, it was no less inevitable that mistaken interpretations should be put forward which needed to be corrected. Nor could the Christian faith be unaffected by the intellectual and moral climates of the ages through which it lived. It had to come to terms with the changing thoughts of the centuries. The task of explaining and defending the Church's faith in Christ is present in every generation and alters in its form as the prevailing wind of secular culture varies. Never was that task more obvious than today.

In this enterprise sometimes one of the classical symbols has been the dominant thought and sometimes the other, but never, I think, one to the exclusion of the other. Both have been needed—the Word and the Son—to expound the full significance of the New Testament revelation. Perhaps, however, it has not always been sufficiently borne in mind that both are symbols and not complete and final statements. They are true, illuminating, and inspired symbols, but they cannot convey the full truth and reality of Christ. So great a mystery as Immanuel, God with us, transcends all human symbols and all human ideas. We know in part.

Two symbols, Son and Word, embody and manifest two aspects of the Incarnation and two reasons for the thankfulness and joy of Christians on the festival of the birth of the Incarnate Lord. We could not do without the revelation of the Son of Man who is also, in a unique sense, the Son of God. The bare assertion that the Divine had become incarnate would be, no doubt, an interesting and indeed momentous philosophical statement, but it would have little power to move our hearts or change our lives.

The Christian faith begins with Jesus of Nazareth and His life and teaching. They were such, His personality was such, that men were driven to ask who He was and led to answer that He was the Messiah, the Son of Man, and, in the end, to think of Him as 'the only begotten of the Father'. Nor can this original insight ever be left behind. It is an essential element in our belief about Christ that He was a real person in history, and that His birth in the 'fullness of time' was an act of God in history.

For this reason Christianity has never been content with an impersonal Deity, it cannot conceive Him as a principle, a substance, a tendency or an idea. He is personal, the supremely personal Being, and He is revealed and mediated to us in the Person Jesus Christ.

The symbol of the Word, though as we have seen in no way superseding that of the Son, embodies a different aspect of the Incarnation. The *Logos* (word) may also mean 'thought', 'reason', or 'wisdom', and it can hardly be imagined that St John was not well aware of this when he wrote 'the Word was made flesh'.

There are various opinions on the question how far Greek philosophy directly influenced the writer of the opening verses of St John's Gospel, but it is a fact that the conception of a divine reason at work in the world was a well-known philosophical theory in the Hellenistic culture. It was an idea which lent itself to the purposes of Christian thinkers, who were eager to commend their faith to educated pagans; it was also a fruitful idea for the development of Christian theology. Once the audacious act of faith had been made which identified Christ with the immanent divine reason in the world, fresh light was gained on the relation of God and the world, and on the divine purpose for the human race.

Like all other creative ideas, this one proved to be less simple than at first appeared and could give rise to doctrines which were out of harmony with fundamental Christian beliefs, but the Church gained one decisive advantage from this insight expressed in 'the Word was made flesh': it placed the Incarnation in a cosmic setting and held forth the Christ as of cosmic significance.

One might say that the Logos doctrine marked the final, and irrevocable, emancipation of the Christian faith from all the limitations of its Hebrew and Jewish origins. The idea is potent still, and we have been given another example of its continued applicability in Teilhard de Chardin's *Le Mileu Divin*, a meditation on the Logos by a devout man of science.

These two aspects of the coming of Christ are each directly relevant to our deepest needs. Who among us has not known the feeling of inner personal loneliness, when life has lost its savour, and even our nearest companions cannot comfort us?

Who has not been on the edge of despair, ready to agree with the pessimist that life itself is vanity, that defeat is our lot and nothing remains worth hoping for?

Moral, intellectual, and physical failure, we almost believe, sum up our life. It is then that the faith in the Son of Man who reveals the Father can come to our rescue. We are not alone. God is no indifferent power or principle. He is like the Lord Jesus Christ, and He loves us each individually, knowing us better than we know ourselves, ready to forgive our past and to bless our future. And sometimes we are invaded by a cosmic despair. The world itself seems to us a vast and complex mechanism, and existence itself, in the end, meaningless.

To cosmic despair the answer is the cosmic Christ. The universe is not a desert, nor is existence purposeless. The eternal Word or Thought of God is in the world, bringing order out of chaos, creation out of destruction, good out of evil, and love out of hate. Not only is He in the world, He is in us, lighting each one and calling each one. We have our parts to play in the divine adventure of the creation and redemption of the world. If that is our faith, we have indeed good reason to rejoice on Christmas Day.

Sunday after Christmas

The ordinary Bible-reader does not concern himself with differences or apparent disagreements between passages unless they are very obvious; he leaves them to be discussed by critics. No doubt this on the whole is a good policy because critical analysis calls for expert knowledge and can be unrewarding for the amateur. Besides, it is so easy to miss the positive significance of Scripture while engrossed in technical puzzles about its text.

In the case of the larger issues raised by the Bible, however, we may make a mistake if we fail to notice the differences and divergencies, for they may well indicate different aspects of the truth, all of which are important.

This is very clearly the case when the question is of the Birth of Christ and His coming into the human world as Saviour. A superficial reading of the New Testament may lead to the conclusion that the Birth is referred to only in the opening of two Gospels, those of Matthew and Luke, and some surprise may be felt that nothing in the rest of the New Testament suggests that the writers were aware of the miraculous events attending Christ's Birth. This impression is partly true, but it is not true that the writers of the other books betray no interest in the Birth. Let us examine this.

The earliest reference to the Birth of Christ, in point of date of writing, is in the Epistle for today, St Paul's letter to the Galatians (4:4–7). The terms are somewhat surprising. 'When the fullness of the time came God sent forth his

Son, born of a woman, born under the law, that he might redeem them who were under the law, that we might receive the adoption of sons.' The intention of the Apostle is to emphasize the real humanity of Jesus. His Birth was that of all mankind and, like them, He was born under some legal system. The purpose of His coming was to set free those who were in that condition so that they might throw off the restrictions of the law and receive the adoption of sons and cry, 'Abba', father, in the Spirit.

It is certainly remarkable that St Paul gives no hint that he knew of miraculous events at the Birth, but it could be said they were not relevant to his argument. More probably, he did not mention them because he did not know about them. There can be no doubt that St Paul believed that the Birth of Christ was a divine act of salvation and that Christ Himself was divine though the relation between the Father and Son had not been thought out.

For St Paul, Christ did not come into existence at Bethlehem: He existed before the foundation of the world: when He came into the world it was as man. When St Paul wrote the Galatian Epistle he thought of Redemption as consisting not only in release from the law but from the dominion of the 'elemental spirits of the universe', to adopt the translation of the New English Bible. What precisely these words mean is not clear, but at least it is evident that, in Paul's belief, Christ had cosmic significance and had been given by the Father the supreme part in the great conflict for the redemption of men.

For our purpose we may take Matthew and Luke together because, although they do not tell the same story, they agree in beginning their Gospels with narratives of the

Birth of Christ. Luke's simple and moving account, whether we hold it to be true or not, has an indisputable place in the literature of the world. A considerable proportion of the New Testament purports to be by the same author and there are good grounds for accepting the claim. Of all the authors of the New Testament we know more about the mind of Luke than that of any other except of St Paul. Paul and Luke were closely associated and the Acts suggests that Luke accompanied Paul on missionary journeys.

Yet these two servants of Christ had different types of mind. One may doubt whether Luke understood or accepted the deeper and more mysterious doctrines of St Paul, for he did not have a restless questioning intellect; his mind was that of a poet rather than that of a mystical philosopher, and his memory and imagination were visual and audile. Perhaps one of the important facts about the New Testament is that Luke was a literary artist, capable of writing in various styles and of masterly concise narrative. The Parable of the Prodigal Son is one of the great short stories in world literature. It is not in any other gospel, and though we may believe it was a story told by Jesus, it was composed in Greek by Luke.

One of the debts we owe to the New English Bible is that it brings out the brilliance of the last eight chapters in Acts, where Luke is writing out of his own mind and vivid memory. In the narrative of the Birth we have the testimony of one who found 'truth embodied in a tale', and he represents a large and important type of personality, consisting of those who 'see' truth and 'feel' it for whom reality is concrete and abstract concepts unreal. I do not know why this manner of thinking should be despised as inferior. Why should it be absurd to hold that the universe is dramatic and that a 'divine comedy' conveys more of reality than any number of equations?

The literature ascribed to 'John' forms a prominent section of the New Testament and has been the subject of innumerable conjectures which cannot be touched on here. If we omit the Book of Revelation as probably by another writer we have material enough to form some opinion of the kind of mind represented by John. It is the not altogether unknown combination of narrative skill with mystical thinking. The Gospel of John includes lively stories, as, for instance, that of the Man Born Blind, but the essence of the book is the spiritual interpretation which follows on the enacted 'signs'.

This Gospel of John is said to have no Birth narrative, and in the normal sense of the words this is true, but in the mind of St John, I believe, the so-called Prologue (John 1:1–18) was the real Birth story. It begins not with the words of the Annunciation to Mary, but with the creation, 'In the beginning was the Word (or Thought)'. The familiar but tremendous sentences describe the Word as being with God and as having part in the creation of the world and as being the life that is the light of men. He was, so this writer asserts, a light to every man, and when He came into the world He came to 'His own', to those who by their inner nature, were capable of responding to Him. To those who, unlike the majority, received Him, He gave the right to become children of God. To John, the word was never completely absent from the world or from the spirits of men: What then is the coming of the Word?

The decisive sentence which separates John from the

Platonic mystics who might have accepted nearly all he wrote about the divine thought, is that which defines the Incarnation: 'The Word became flesh and dwelt among us, full of grace and truth.' In John's understanding of the gospel, the birth of Christ was both the most stupendous of miracles, comparable only with the Creation, and also the most natural of events, for it was the manifestation of the nature of God and the consummation of the central element in the nature of man.

From that point of view perhaps the details of the infant who was the Incarnate Word might seem relatively unimportant, and I think it would be precarious to proclaim that John must have held either the virgin Birth or the completely 'natural' Birth of the Lord: both could be in harmony with his central belief that the Word was made Flesh. If, as is probable, John is to be identified with 'the disciple whom Jesus loved' there may be some significance in the words from the cross, 'When Jesus saw his mother and the disciple standing by whom he loved, he said to his mother, Woman, behold thy son. Then he said to the disciple, Behold thy mother! And from that hour the disciple took her unto his own home.' (John 19:26f.)

These presentations of the birth of Christ are different but not mutually exclusive. St Luke, for example, chooses the form of a story, 'Once upon a time'; St John does not contradict but takes the story beyond one time to every time, giving it the dimension of eternity, helping us to understand that the coming of Christ is a present reality. Now He comes to us who are His own and to as many as receive Him He gives the right to share His Sonship and become Children of God.

Epiphany

The Collect for Epiphany aptly sums up the spiritual meaning of the story of Wise Men who, led by their astrological beliefs, came to the cradle of the Son of God. We are taught to pray that our knowledge of God 'by faith' may bring us to 'fruition', that is to the direct knowledge which theologians have described as the Vision of God. The fruition, says the Collect, comes 'after this life', but though the New Testament doubtless indicates that the perfect knowledge of God can be only in the 'life of the world to come' it also teaches that 'eternal life' which consists in the knowledge of God, can begin now.

The life of faith, then, is a venture in search of knowledge. According to this parable we who have faith are acting on the basis of principles of which we are not certain. The Wise Men took a risk that their astrological conjectures might be mistaken and the guidance of the star an illusion. If it is thus in our own spiritual life, we may encourage ourselves by observing that all searches for truth begin with an act of faith, or at least as a venture the outcome of which is uncertain, and if to know God has its risks, so has our attempt to know our friends.

To become really friendly with another person I must assume, at least as a working hypothesis, that he is worth knowing and that knowing him is not completely impossible. I suppose no human friendship has ever been perfect. There has never been one entirely without set-backs and in this world never have two persons known each other without reservation. Indeed, good friends as we may be, do we really want to be perfectly known, or to know perfectly the mind of our friend? Knowledge of our closest human friend must be imperfect, but it can be real and can be increasing day by day. The limit to our knowledge of him may be set by our friend himself who says, as he has every right to do, 'Thus far and no further do I admit you to the secret places of my heart.' God, so St Paul believed, puts no limit to our progress in knowledge of Him; we may hope to 'know even as we are known' (1 Corinthians 13:12).

One final reflection demands to be heard. Most of us will think that in fact the Wise Men were mistaken from the start because astrology is a false science. It is not unknown in human friendships that they may begin in misunderstanding and end in love. Perhaps the Wise Men owed their revelation not to the stars but to their ardent desire and their readiness to venture.

First Sunday after Epiphany

A GROWING BOY

The one glimpse which we have of Jesus between His Birth and His public ministry is St Luke's account of His adventure at the age of twelve when He stayed behind in the Temple to ask questions of the learned men (Luke 2:41–52). The main purpose of the Evangelist seems to be to emphasize that Jesus grew up like any other boy, increasing in height and also in 'wisdom', but we are given too a hint that there was a certain tension in His relation with His parents who did not understand Him—a not uncommon experience in the process of growing up. The life of Jesus was truly human in all its phases.

The powerful attraction of this story, however, arises from the belief that Jesus, while truly human, was also the Incarnate Son of God. John Colet, when he founded St Paul's School, composed a Latin prayer for its scholars addressed to the Boy Jesus and arranged that an image of Christ as a boy should stand above the High Master's chair. Was Colet wrong in praying to the Boy Jesus as though He was still twelve years old? Ought he to have said in his prayer, 'Thou who wast once a boy,' implying that He was so no longer? Colet was an orthodox Christian and knew what he was doing. The life of Jesus was, he believed, more than an ordinary human life; it was at every stage a manifestation of the life of God, of the Eternal Being, of the Divine nature. And, therefore, all Christ's human experiences had the tincture of eternity; unlike our experiences they did not persist only as memories but were themselves eternal.

And this is a truth which affects us in our devotional practice. We are justified when, as at this season, we worship the Babe of Bethlehem or the growing Boy in the Temple. We can understand too the saying of Pascal, 'Christ has been in agony from the foundation of the world', for all the experiences of Jesus in His earthly life are reflections of the life of God. We may think of Him, and adore Him, as child, adolescent, carpenter, teacher, prophet, healer, persecuted outcast, condemned criminal, crucified, risen and glorified. Nay, we must think of Him in all these aspects, for all of them together compose the reality with which we have to do. Some of these pictures of Christ are more important than others. Christ on the cross means more than Christ in the cradle but even exclusive concentration on the Man on the Cross is misleading; we need to know the career that led to Gethsemane and Calvary and to the overcoming of death. To observe the Christian year with its calendar, which marks the salient events in the earthly life of Jesus, helps to ensure that we neglect nothing which we ought to include in our picture of our Lord. I think we owe to the Puritans the expression 'the whole process of the Christ'; it is a good phrase, whoever coined it, so long as we add that the process is not like those in which the stages are ephemeral, and interesting only as leading to the end of the development. In this process each stage is a disclosure of reality and truth, including that of the growing Boy who asked questions in the Temple so long ago.

Second Sunday after Epiphany

THE PEACEMAKERS

'Grant us thy peace all the days of our life.' There was a time when some vigorous persons complained that our Prayer Book was too full of fear and taught us to pray too often for security and peace. That was when it could be imagined that peace was the normal condition of the world and war only a remote possibility. In these days, when what peace there is hangs to a large extent on a balance of fear, there can be few who will not echo the words of the Collect for today.

We pray for peace on the assumption that God is the author and giver of peace, and that it is his peace that we need. But who are we that offer the prayer? We are children of God in Christ's Church, and mindful, let us hope, of the words of our Master who said, 'Blessed are the peacemakers, for they shall be called sons of God.' We are hypocrites when we pray for peace, if we are not trying also to make it.

Anyone who reads the Bible right through must be aware of a certain strangeness in the various representations of God which it contains. Sometimes He is called the 'Lord of Hosts', and even the 'God of Battles', who leads the Hebrews in their conquest, and massacre, of the tribes of Canaan—the very opposite of the God of Peace. It is indeed a strange and wonderful thing that the tribal deity of a Semitic people should, so to say, have become the God and Father of our Lord Jesus Christ; but it has happened, and within the Old Testament we have testimony that the experience of the Prophets caused them to declare that God was the source of justice and harmony, continually at work overcoming chaos, division, and strife.

'God is a righteous judge, strong and patient, and God is provoked every day', writes the Psalmist, stating, we may think, in a few words some of the attributes necessary for peace-making. Unless we have an idea of justice which we revere we cannot begin the task, for so long as we regard the situation as simply a clash of interests we are just one of the contenders with no higher aim than to see that our interests prevail. We must at least desire that everyone, as far as possible, should have his due, even if we suffer loss. And anyone who has essayed the task of making peace will know how much patience is required, how hard it is to keep one's temper in face of obstinate unreason. 'Lord, give me patience', must be our prayer.

In the light of the gospel we add one more needed quality, and that the most important of all—love in the form of compassion. Idealists are prone to forget that they are concerned with sinful and fallible mortal men who need the grace of God to rise above the normal selfish impulses of humanity. The idealists should not forget because, if they look into themselves, they will find these same impulses just beneath the surface. After all, we have still left out one quality of the peacemaker—he will be more likely to succeed if he is at peace within himself and at peace with God.

THE CONCEIT OF WISDOM

'Be not wise in your own conceits.' The opening words of today's Epistle (Romans 12:16–21) convey a piece of advice which everyone will recognize as good, except perhaps in his own case.

The Greek word does not imply, as the English 'conceit' might do, that the Apostle is thinking only of crotchety or cranky individuals; they mean literally, 'Be not wise with yourselves', that is, I suppose, without reference to any opinions other than your own.

St Paul is writing about the conduct of Christians in the fellowship of the Church and he develops this theme with the guiding thought that 'charity', *agape*, loving kindness, is the principal thought which should govern all thoughts and actions.

The man who is wise 'with himself' forgets or despises the brethren who are members of the one Body of Christ and, as an ancient Father has remarked, anyone who venerates his own stupidity as if it were wisdom can hardly know the wisdom of God.

What kind of person was before Paul's imagination when he wrote these words? Probably those well-meaning but tiresome individuals in Corinth and elsewhere who caused trouble by fantastic speculations on divine things or engendered divisions by unreasonable partisanship—those who cried, 'I am on Paul's side', or 'I am for Apollos'. Such persons endangered the unity of the Spirit in the bond of peace.

To be humble about one's own wisdom, like all humility, is a difficult virtue and has a special problem of its own. What are the limits of humility here? Obviously there are occasions when deference to the opinions of others ought to be superseded and we have to maintain against them what we hold to be the truth. Doubtless we have reason to regret that sometimes we ignored the advice of our friends, but have we not also regretted sometimes that we did not rely on our own judgement?

St Paul certainly did not intend to recommend unlimited deference to the opinions of others, or, if he did, he condemned himself, for he did not hesitate to oppose no less a person than St Peter when he was sure that he had the wisdom of God and St Peter had not. In that memorable dispute much was at stake—the whole future of the Church —but in less momentous affairs similar situations arise and we have to take our stand.

Not even an Apostle can give us a rule that will decide things for us; we have to make our own decision; but he can tell us the conditions in which we may hope to act Christianly. Our wisdom must have taken into account the Body of Christ and its members; it must have been developed in charity and free from all taint of pride or personal feelings; it must be, so far as we are able to discover, the expression of truth.

It will do us no harm if we remember the words of Oliver Cromwell addressed to Christian men who were sure they were right: 'I beseech you, in the bowels of Christ, to think it possible you may be mistaken.'

Fourth Sunday after Epiphany

POWER OF THE PAST

Though we live in the present, the past and the future enter into all our experiences. The Collect for today can serve as an illustration.

It begins by stating that we 'live in the midst of so many and great dangers, that by reason of the frailty of our nature we cannot always stand upright'—the memory of past experience—and it goes on to pray for 'strength and protection' in the dangers and temptations of the future.

There is a sense in which it could be said that we are our past. Memory is the link which most clearly demonstrates to us that we are the same individuals as we were in years gone by. Philosophers have indeed debated whether we can conceive personal identity apart from some continuity of memories.

We cannot cut ourselves off from our past, but we must hesitate to admit that our past is the whole explanation, or complete account, of what we are, for if we did make that assertion, we should be denying that we had any freedom of choice in the present. We should be the slaves of the past.

Thus there are occasions when we rightly attempt to forget the past. We can never do that quite literally so long as we remain sane, but we can at least make an effort to counteract the influences and memories which come from former days.

St Paul put this emphatically. He describes his own mental and physical attitude as 'forgetting those things that are behind and stretching out towards those that are before' (Philippians 3:13).

He did not mean that his mind had become a blank, or that he did not recollect the time when he was a 'Pharisee of the Pharisees'. When he wrote these words he had actually been referring to his former life. He meant that he did not dwell on these memories; he did not live in the past, from which in fact he had so far as possible dissociated himself. He had some more urgent business with the future.

To institutions and to persons the power of the past and the call of the future are inescapable realities. The Church is an institution, though not a merely human one. She too must, in some measure. live in the past and by memories. What happened in Palestine long ago is of the deepest concern to her, and if she lost her recollection of the historical Jesus and His words and deeds she would lose her identity. But she dare not live in the past entirely. She has business, urgent business, in the present and the future.

One may sometimes fear that the power of the past in Christian action is too great. We search the records for precedents before we will embark on any new venture or express the gospel in unaccustomed words.

In this caution we are not apostolic, though we may be looking for apostolic precedents. It was the Apostle Paul who was willing to forget the past so that he might gain the future; it was the Apostle John who conveyed to us the promise of the Holy Spirit, who would interpret the meaning of Christ to every age.

Christianity is indeed an historical religion indissolubly linked with past events—but its eyes are turned to the future, and its inspiration lies, not in nostalgic memories, but in hope of the Kingdom of God.

Fifth Sunday after Epiphany

DUALISM

Some recent writers refer to 'Christian Dualism' and among the New Testament references which seem to justify them is the Parable of the Tares, which forms the Gospel for today (Matthew 13:24–30). The story of a malicious enemy who sowed weeds in a farmer's wheat is adduced to illustrate the Kingdom of Heaven.

Christianity is usually reckoned as one of the mono-theistic faiths, which also has impressive support in the New Testament. A standing problem for Christian thinkers must be how to reconcile the doctrine that there is only one God with the plain indications in the Gospels that Jesus believed there was a real conflict between the Heavenly Father and an 'enemy'. If we take the Parable of the Tares seriously, it would imply that the 'enemy' can work mischief which takes God by surprise.

To go further into the question is no task for a brief essay, but one can put into a very few words a warning against neglecting the elements of 'dualism' in the New Testament. A hasty conclusion that it must be a mistake, or a concession to undeveloped minds, has led to confusion on the subject of evil and suffering. It seems that if God is one and infinite and good He cannot have caused or permitted any real evil, and all too easily we can infer from this that what appears as evil to us is really good.

In the mind of Jesus suffering and sin were alike the work of the enemy who had to be overcome by the power of

God. Perhaps it would be more accurate to describe the 'dualism' of Christianity as 'interim dualism'.

Certainly St Paul is not a thoroughgoing dualist, for he would violently reject any hint that there are two more or less equal principles or powers at work, but he does believe in the temporary initiative of evil spirits. His monotheism is achieved in the future, when, after the victory of Christ, God shall be all in all. Paul's monotheism has one great advantage over versions of belief in only one God which omit the time factor. Whereas a man who believes that at this moment God is 'all in all' can hardly feel that he is called upon to improve the situation, one who believes that God is recruiting soldiers in the campaign for the kingdom of justice, love, and joy has a cause to serve and strength to endure.

Sixth Sunday after Epiphany

VITAL DIFFERENCE

St John's presentation of the gospel is dominated by pairs of opposites, which are also alternatives for our choice. Life and death, light and darkness are two such pairs which are plain enough to any reader, but in today's Epistle (I John 3:1–8) we have a pair which is perhaps not so obvious —that of destruction and creation.

The love of the Father, revealed in Christ, we are told, has brought into being men and women who are 'sons of God', and in the same breath, as it were, we are informed that the Son of God 'was manifested to destroy the works of the devil'. The one and the same Christ both destroys and creates; yet there is a vital difference which we must note: the creation is of new persons, persons born again, but the destruction is not of persons, but of 'works'. He does not destroy the devil's children, for the devil has no children. He destroys the devil's work by changing those whom it had perverted into sons of God. The creation is the destruction.

The world wars of this troubled century were, as most of us believe, waged against evils which could be described as 'works of the devil', and, up to a point, they halted the march of arrogant wickedness. They destroyed some of the instruments and strongholds of the enemy, but did they do much more? Did they 'make the world safe for democracy', or for anything else that we value? We know that they did not. So far, the signs of a better, happier, and more just civilization emerging from destruction are not easily discernible. Yet we should be traitors to the cause of humanity if we gave up hope and resolution; the old order, which gave scope for the devil's works, will not be finally destroyed until the new order has been created.

This principle of destruction through creation permeates the whole of human life, international, national, and individual. In every sphere simply to be against evil is largely futile, and righteous indignation without positive ideals can have, at the best, only a limited effect. And that applies to ourselves in our private and secret experience. We may feel angry with ourselves, or disgusted, or even hate ourselves but what we react against in ourselves can be destroyed only by a creative power which changes our personalities, a new dominating purpose which alters the focus of our attention. As St John puts it in his antithetical manner, the works of the devil in us will be destroyed in proportion as we can say truly, 'Now are we sons of God.'

Septuagesima

The story of creation, which is the first lesson for the morning of Septuagesima Sunday, awakens questions in modern and attentive minds, but it will be a pity if we allow our interest in the details of the Genesis narrative to avert our attention from the one really important point—the assertion that all things depend ultimately on God.

The first words of the Bible are a proclamation of Monotheism.

Although we read in Genesis that the Creator rested on the seventh day we should misinterpret its meaning if we supposed that the Divine activity was only 'in the beginning'. The Bible is very far from suggesting that the Creator lost interest in His creation. We are to think of Him as sustaining all things and directing the course of events by His Providence.

'God is working His purpose out as year succeeds to year': the words of the hymn express a central conviction of Christians and one to which for our soul's health we need to hold fast. It is the answer, too, of revelation to the mood of pessimism when we are tempted to cry: 'There is no meaning in existence or in our human lives.' The meaning is the divine purpose, which, in part, we are able to understand and either to further or to hinder, and our high privilege is to be workers together with God.

It is interesting to notice that the Communists have a secular imitation of the doctrine of Providence in their theory of the 'historical line', which seems to signify the inevitable trend of history. And I suppose that something like the inspiration which Christians derive from their belief that they can be fellow-workers with God may come to a Marxist when he feels that he is moving with the flowing tide of the dialectic of history.

It is interesting, too, that a difficulty arises for the Communist which has often been a trouble to reflective Christians. The Communist may logically ask why he should exert himself when the historical line will work itself out whatever he does or does not do. So the Christian also might wonder whether the Providence of God needs any assistance from him. I don't know what the Communist would reply; I doubt whether there is an answer; but the Christian reply does, at least in principle, meet the objection. We shall say surely that a major element in the divine purpose is to bring into being free persons who are capable of choice between good and evil and, in this respect, images of their Creator.

The chapters of Genesis which follow the Creation story show, as it were in a parable, the purpose of God frustrated by the self-will of His creatures and they hint at the providential plan of redemption by which evil may be overcome with good while preserving that human freedom which is the basis of man's dignity.

God's strategy in the face of the rebellion of His creatures is not to reduce them to slaves or puppets who are incapable of rejecting His laws, but to make them sons who are in harmony with His will.

Sexagesima

THE TRAMPLED EARTH

The Parable of the Sower is recorded in all of the first three Gospels and there are echoes of it in the Gospel of John. When we hear it today in St Luke's version, as the Gospel for Sexagesima (Luke 8:4–15), we shall notice that it includes an interpretation, attributed to Jesus, given to the disciples.

Modern commentators are inclined to doubt this attribution and, whatever we may think about this question of criticism, it seems to me that the explanation of the seed that fell by the wayside needs to be supplemented.

Some seed, we read, fell by the wayside and was trodden down so that the birds devoured it. The birds had their opportunity because of the nature of the soil which was trampled by the feet of passers-by.

We have surely here a picture of a man who is so entangled with the affairs of the day and so weighed down by the urgent trivialities of business and family that 'the Word', the message of the Kingdom, never penetrates below the surface of his mind. The man is not anxious or unhappy—he is simply always involved and busy, with, he supposes, no time to think of what he is here for or the purpose of his busyness. In other words, he lacks leisure.

We are promised that, if all goes well, we shall have abundant leisure in the days to come as the Welfare State gets into its stride, and there are discussions of how we can train ourselves, or perhaps more often others, to use this leisure.

Somewhat paradoxically, the suggestions put forward seem to aim at disguising leisure as work, voluntary activities of a worthy kind which will fill up the otherwise empty time.

No one would deny that all this is useful and praise-worthy, but it does not solve the problem of leisure. We are at leisure when we have nothing to do, when no tasks demand our attention either imposed or voluntary. A man who has no vacant hours would not know what leisure is.

We were taught in our childhood that Satan has mischief for idle hands to do, and how true that homely admonition is, but it is also true that God can speak His word to us when we are at leisure.

'Contemplation' is a formidable word which calls up in our imagination saints and philosophers, but the activity of contemplation is quite simple. We begin by thinking in a detached way about the fundamental realities of our existence, of our lives, and of our death, of the being of God and the promises of Christ.

If we allow ourselves leisure to think properly, we shall soon find ourselves in perplexity and discover that we our-selves are a riddle. Then it may be, the Word of the King-dom will come home to us. At the very least, we shall have some inkling of what religion is all about.

The trampled earth is only one instance; other kinds of earth are mentioned in the parable. All of them are con-sidered in their relation to the seed and only in the good earth does the seed survive.

Quinquagesima

Every year, on the Sunday before Lent begins, we are called to listen to the wonderful paean in praise of love, which is the highest achievement of St Paul's literary genius and the most illuminating expression of his personal religion (I Corinthians 13). It has rightly been designated a hymn, and the beauty of the poetry enchants us. But it is more than a 'very pleasant song'; we shall miss its meaning if we do not recognize that it is a careful statement of a moral principle and ideal. An ethical theory is implied—one that puts 'love' at the centre of the idea of good rather than justice—and we are given a picture of the perfect Christian individual.

The modern translations of the New Testament have made the characteristics of the love-inspired individual more definite and specific than they were in the older versions. We shall hear, for example, if the Prayer Book is adhered to, that love 'thinketh no evil', which is somewhat vague. The better knowledge which scholars now possess of the vocabulary of the Greek which St Paul wrote enables them to be more explicit. A brilliant translation in the New English Bible brings out St Paul's meaning, 'Love keeps no score of wrongs'. This is quite a different, and more appropriate, sense. St Paul is not saying that love never thinks about evil, which would be a doubtful virtue, for it could hardly be praiseworthy to disregard the evil in the world. The situation which is in view is that of a man who has suffered wrongs and has real cause for resentment. The natural man will keep account of his injuries, and perhaps bide his time to retaliate—as we say 'to make the score even'. The man who has Christian love in his heart will not keep the score. This does not mean that he will be indifferent to justice; he will have 'indignation against successful vice', but all thoughts of personal revenge will be banished and his fight against justice will be free from all selfish partiality.

From the standpoint of the individual, the advice not to keep the score is plainly excellent. On the lowest ground, to harbour resentment and to be constantly reminding oneself of one's wrongs is a source of weakness and distraction from the real business of living. From the spiritual point of view, the nourishment of hatred is devastating and diverts us from the love of God. We must forgive if we would be forgiven.

On a larger view, the wiping out of scores is surely one of the most urgent needs of humanity at the present time. Atrocious wrongs have been done. Their memory cannot be obliterated, but the memory must not dominate actions. If large sections of the human race are intent on 'paying off old scores', we shall never be in sight of peace. St Paul's song of love is the programme of 'pure and peaceable wisdom'.

Ash Wednesday

There is no merit in making oneself miserable, and any self-denial we may practise in matters of food during Lent is properly designed to help us to have a 'time of refreshing from the Lord', spiritual release and joy.

It is a time to feed our souls. And how shall we do that better than by meditating on the Word of God?

Though of course we must think of ourselves and of our sins of commission and omission, we are not to dwell over much on that depressing subject; rather we are to look away from ourselves to God revealed in Christ.

How many, even among convinced Christians, have read right through the New Testament as a single exercise and act of devotion? It could easily be done before Easter, and is worth the effort, but to get the greatest benefit we ought to have a theme or interest to guide our thoughts.

I suggest that, since the New Testament as a whole, is about Christ, we might well consider each book from the point of view of what it has to tell us about Him, with the aim of bringing our minds and imaginations into harmony with our Lord.

Just to read the New Testament through as it stands would be of inestimable advantage, but we should be wise to change the order in our reading so as to gain an impression of the continuity of the New Testament revelation.

Naturally we shall begin with the Gospels and first of all

with the Gospel of St Mark, which is the primary authority for the life of Jesus, and pass on to the Gospels of Matthew and Luke, and add to the record of His teaching information of transcendent importance.

Then, if we take the advice of many commentators, we should read the Acts of the Apostles, not staying to study the many interesting historical questions which the book raises, but observing the growth of the Church and the deepening of its understanding of the Christ.

From then onwards we come to books which, as it were, present to us various aspects of Christ and interpretations of His work and Person; we can note the fundamental agreement of the writers and the differences of their individual experiences and presentations.

At the end, perhaps, we should read the Gospel of John and ask ourselves whether in it we have the most profound interpretation of the Christ whom we had first met in the simple pages of Mark.

By the time Easter has come we should be ready to embark on the mysterious and magnificent book of Revelation with its poetical and prophetic proclamation of the conquest of evil by Him who was dead and is alive for evermore.

No one can predict what the effect of such a reading will be on another man. It is conceivable that he will reject the whole as legendary illusion, but it is more likely, I think, that he will feel at least that here is mystery and also deep and searching reality.

First Sunday in Lent

FASTING

Today's Gospel tells us that, at the outset of His ministry, Jesus fasted for forty days in the wilderness (Matthew 4). It is evident, too, that He expected His followers to fast; for He warns them against doing it 'like the hypocrites'. Fasting, therefore, has a place in the Christian life, and we may reasonably ask, What place, and why?

With regard to the pleasures of the body there are two extreme views and practices. All moralists, and every spiritual religion, dwell upon the danger of sensualism, the former as corrupting the higher faculties of the self, the latter as leading to the separation of the soul from God. The thoroughgoing ascetics have exaggerated these truths to the extent of actually regarding pleasure as evil in itself.

It needs no argument to show that the New Testament condemns the sensualist as a kind of idolator whose 'God is his belly', but it is important to note that it never suggests that pleasure is evil. Our Lord was not among those 'who appear unto men to fast', for His enemies accused Him of being 'a gluttonous man and a wine-bibber' and we have evidence in the Gospels that He was a welcome guest at feasts. He was no gloomy kill-joy, and though the Epistles abound in denunciations of the licentious customs of pagan social life, they assume that joy and pleasure are good and that God 'gives us all things richly to enjoy'.

The rationale of fasting is given succinctly by St Paul when he writes, 'All things are lawful for me, but I will not be brought under the power of any', and goes on to remind us of the evanescent nature of bodily pleasure, 'Meats for the belly and the belly for meats, but God shall bring to naught both it and them' (I Corinthians 6:12f.). How can anyone whose joys are all dependent on the mortal body be a partaker of eternal life?

Are we being brought under the power of any pleasure or satisfaction which is lawful in itself but hinders our spiritual development? In trying to answer this question we should look beyond the obvious physical pleasures and include others which have an element of intellectual activity. Perhaps this is not the appropriate place to mention excessive reading of newspapers, but we can spend time on them which might be better employed. Is it unknown that some have fallen under the power of television? A time of fasting will be well spent if we use it to regain control of ourselves by the grace of God. What are the priorities in our lives? What are the dearest sources of pleasure and satisfaction to us? And, most inclusive of all, have we installed the belly, or some more respectable disguise of it, as an idol in the room of God?

Second Sunday in Lent

PILFERING

A much-travelled friend for certain purposes divides countries into two classes: the first, those in which you can be fairly certain that persons you deal with are not trying to cheat you; and the second, those in which it is advisable to count your change very carefully. When last I met him he said he was thinking of moving this country from the first to the second class. Perhaps he had some unfortunate experience which he has wrongly taken as typical, but quite possibly he is judging realistically. The losses due to theft, much of it petty, what the Catechism calls 'picking and stealing', mount up to quite staggering sums and seriously affect the national economy.

My friend is inclined to attribute the decline in honesty to the fading of a belief in hell. I think that is too crude, but is nevertheless partly true. A weakening of belief in God is almost certain to lead to a weakening of the sense of obligation. Let no one interpret this as meaning that unbelievers have no ethics or are necessarily wicked; what I say is that a change from genuine belief in God to disbelief is likely to lead to a deterioration in conduct. The man who believed in God believed in two things which are implied in the idea of God—an objective standard and an objective judge. The code of conduct which he accepted was not invented by himself, nor was it a creation of public opinion. It did not depend on a majority vote; it was based on the nature of things, on the will of God. The judgement on his conduct in like manner was not the opinion of 'his better self', or of 'the men of good will', nor can it be deceived by appearances; it is the judgement of omniscience, and it is always going on.

When this same man ceases to believe in God he is at a loss to conceive how any standard of conduct can be objective or rise above the status of mere opinion, and he cannot imagine any judgement on himself and his conduct which is higher than his own judgement or that of persons like himself. When such a man finds himself in a situation where there is practically no danger of discovery, where public opinion will not have any chance of expression, will he not more easily persuade himself that the law against stealing is irrational, a defence perhaps of the ill-gotten gains of capitalists, not to be taken seriously by intelligent and spirited persons? So integrity and truth are dissolved in dialectic.

'As God is my judge': 'Thou God seest me'; these two phrases which used to be much in the minds of our pious grandparents, are not dwelt upon now and of course, taken by themselves, they are no basis for a full Christian life. Yet they crystallize two beliefs which have given iron to the will of many tempted souls. God is my judge, and He alone; and His eyes are always upon me.

Third Sunday in Lent

NOT AN OBSESSION

If we listen to the Gospel today we shall find ourselves in a somewhat queer country (Luke 11:14–28). We shall hear about the casting out of a devil of dumbness and a story of how an 'unclean spirit', having left a man, returns and, finding his former abode empty, brings in seven other devils. We may conjecture that this is Jesus' comment on a case where His healing power did not effect a permanent cure. In addition, we shall hear an emphatic statement by Jesus that His authority over demons was an evidence that, with Him, the Kingdom of God had come.

A fundamental question is, what possession by an 'unclean spirit' means in modern terms. Probably we should describe the condition as a compulsive obsession which drove the patient to the satisfaction of desires and instincts which normal individuals control. The 'driving out' of the demon is a picture of the effect of an encounter with Jesus, which broke down the obsession and liberated the personality of the sufferer. But what shall we say about the relapse, the return of the unclean spirit? The point of the story, as told by our Lord, is that the house was empty; the vacancy was there to be occupied. We could translate this into modern terms, at least in part, by supposing that the patient, when his obsessions had been dissolved, was left without any motive force, lacking direction and interest. Formerly dominated by irrational and compulsive drives, now he is hopelessly adrift.

Does he need another obsession of a superior type? I have read somewhere the statement that St Paul was 'obsessed' by Christ. This is perhaps one way of emphasizing the Apostle's absolute devotion to his Lord, but I think it is mistaken. St Paul felt 'constrained' by the love of Christ, but this was totally different from the compulsion of an obsession. An obsessed individual narrows his mind and his imagination, his emotions are inhumanly limited, and his affections withered. He is disintegrating. Precisely the opposite was the result of his alleged 'obsession' in the case of Paul. His faith and devotion pervaded his whole being and quickened every faculty, intellect, imagination, emotions and affection. We need another word to describe him and all who, like him, have left obsessions behind in the power of Christ and have found freedom. The word is 'focus'. An obsession produces a dreadful unity by eliminating most of the values of life; a focus unifies while enhancing them.

Unlike an obsession a focus needs attention and adjustment, for it does not destroy our freedom, and almost unaware we may get our lives and ourselves out of focus. But the great thing is that we should know where our sanity and spiritual health lie. It is not enough to straighten out our psychological kinks, or put our mental confusions in order, to 'sweep and garnish' the house; an empty mind, and an empty heart, are vulnerable.

Fourth Sunday in Lent

PUNISHMENT DESERVED

The Collect for the Fourth Sunday in Lent may seem to the sophisticated intolerably childish, and it must be owned that it speaks a language which many of us understood better in the nursery then we do now. We are invited to acknowledge that we 'worthily deserve to be punished' and to ask quite simply that we may be let off the penalty. Subtle questions can be raised about the meaning of personal guilt and how far the 'evil deeds' which are alleged to demand retribution are really our deeds. On that point it may be enough to remark that few would be content to agree that they are not responsible beings, and in fact if we are not responsible at all it would seem that all discussion of religion, ethics, politics and most other human concerns must be a waste of time.

But what shall we think about punishment? The prayer evidently means retribution and not simply salutary discipline, it envisages some pain or loss visited upon us just because we deserve it, and which will follow on our sins whether it has the effect of improving our characters or not.

In current discussions of punishment the retributive theory has fallen into disrepute and perhaps this is well when we are thinking of the imperfect justice of human judges, but the Bible, which is concerned with justice, certainly includes retribution in the conception of punishment. The objection which is made that vengeance is attributed to God by such expressions and that revenge cannot be reconciled with the faith that He is love is really wide of the mark. The creation which depends on a holy Creator must be a moral order, and this involves that, in the end, the evil will is always defeated. To desire that this should be so is a natural impulse of the human heart.

When we encounter insolent examples of successful vice we feel that the world would be a quieter place if the wrongdoers were exposed and humiliated. If we are Christians we shall hope, too, that they will be converted and reformed, but that does not in any way diminish our natural desire that justice should be done.

Anger is nearly always a dangerous emotion and to give rein to it sinful—but not always; a lack of indignation against successful vice may be a contemptible sluggishness of conscience. The Gospels present to us the person of our Lord as meek and lowly and full of compassion, but they show Him, too, as one whose anger blazed against evil deeds done to His Father's weaker children. It is right to be indignant against successful vice. But suppose that the vice is my own, will my indignation turn against myself? If I am honest, it will, and I may hope through repentance to turn away the wrath of God.

Passion Sunday

◇◇◇◇◇◇◇◇◇◇◇◇◇◇◇◇◇◇◇◇◇◇◇※◇◇◇◇◇◇◇◇◇◇◇◇◇◇◇◇◇◇◇◇◇◇◇

WHOSE FAULT?

On Passion Sunday the Church invites us to begin to turn our thoughts definitely on the Crucifixion of our Lord—that stone of stumbling to so many, and rock of salvation to so many more. We may try to make the event and the central Figure vivid in our imagination: we may even, though with fear, strive to enter into the thoughts of the Crucified.

Considered as history and as a human tragedy there is much in the Crucifixion to stir up reflection and to pierce our normal complacency. One question is bound to arise when we reflect—who was chiefly responsible? It is still debated, but we may reasonably suppose that in this case of atrocious injustice, as in so many others, though some were originating agents, the guilt was more widely spread, and many who took no ostensible part contributed to the crime, perhaps by their inaction and by simply 'minding their own business'.

But, if we are Christian believers, we cannot rest on this historical level. We pass on to the level of faith and its insight, and we see in the Passion far more than the deplorable and pathetic death of a hero. We see the sacrifice of the Son of God manifesting the divine judgement on sin, and the eternal love which forgives the repentant sinner offering him reconciliation and eternal life.

In J. S. Bach's St Matthew Passion there is a moment which touches the quick of Christian devotion. It occurs after the chorus 'Lord is it I?' which is followed by the chorale 'My sin it was which bound thee, which did with woes surround thee, and nailed thee to the tree'. That is the deepest answer to the question, Whose fault? The Saviour came to be a sacrifice for the sin of the whole world, for all men and to redeem them—including me.

This personal and individual relation with the Saviour is inescapable in the New Testament and in Christian experience ever since. 'He loved me and gave himself up for me', says St Paul, and we can hear the wonder and the gratitude in those simple words. They are at the heart of the gospel.

The revelation of the love of God in the passion of Christ is, in one sense, a mystery, for we cannot prove it by scientific reason nor can we fully understand its necessity, though human analogies help us to catch some gleam of the divine wisdom. We feel the reality and the power without clearly comprehending.

One thing is plain—the answer of the gospel of redemption to human needs. And never more plain than now. For we are forgetting the weight and guilt of sin, but we don't get rid of it by forgetting, nor of its consequences, and we are losing hope in any blessed future for ourselves and for humanity.

In devout contemplation of the Passion we may discover a new seriousness in our daily lives and a new inspiration for living them. Through meditation on the Cross may we be brought to repentance and hope.

Palm Sunday

MADE A SLAVE

Though the translation of the Epistle for Palm Sunday (Philippians 2:5–11) in the New English Bible falls below the majesty of the older version, it probably brings out the meaning more clearly. St Paul is describing the Christian life as an imitation of Christ, but he does not dwell on the example of the historical Jesus as much as on the humiliation of the Son of God. Though His nature was divine, He 'made himself nothing, assuming the nature of a slave', of a servant who drew no wages. We remember that Jesus said much the same thing about Himself; the Son of Man came not to be served, but to serve. This voluntary humility with the purpose of giving service or help is the pattern of our life in Christ.

From this arises a plain and straightforward question which we can easily put to ourselves. What are our estimates of value? Do we admire the proud and despise the humble? Or, coming closer to the core of the matter, what are our dominant motives, and on what episodes in our existence do we think with most satisfaction? If we have to confess that the Ego has been our constant centre, and all that conduced to its imagined well-being and complacency our source of pleasure, we are, alas, far off the beam; if, on the contrary, we can think with thankful warmth of deeds which served others at some sacrifice to ourselves, we may believe that our minds are not wholly cut off and alien to the mind of Christ.

To act consistently on this principle involves renunciation of some pleasant experiences and may lead us to suffer pain which prudent selfishness would have avoided; for Jesus the path led to utter loneliness, rejection and agonizing death; but the note of the gospel of Christ is not gloom, but joy.

The earthly life of the Son of Man was lighted by the love and gratitude of those whom He healed, or some of them, by the affection of friends and the laughter of children. He rejoiced in the beauty of nature and the companionship of common people, and we are told that it was 'for the joy set before him' that He endured the cross, despising the shame.

Many of us must have wondered at the cheerfulness of nurses, who are so grossly overworked and underpaid. At one time I thought, rather cynically perhaps, that the cheerfulness was a part of the professional technique, like the fixed smiles of ballet dancers. But I have learned a better answer. At the end of every turn of duty by day or night they can say, 'Everything I have done has been an act of service to afflicted persons. Everything has been worth while and nothing wasted.' In our confused and madly acquisitive society there are not many of us who can answer questions posed by the Epistle with so little shame.

Monday in Holy Week

HOLY WEEK THOUGHTS

This Holy Week will no doubt be like other Holy Weeks, a time when the few will remember the passion of the Lord and the many will bestow only a passing thought upon it and treat Good Friday as an ordinary holiday.

Some of these will be persons who are not accustomed to thinking seriously about anything, but others will be real unbelievers who have decided that the Christian faith about Christ is not true. Even so I suggest they would be well advised to remember why Good Friday is not only a holiday but a Holy day.

Though they may think that Jesus died for an illusion, they can read the account of His death, as they read Plato's account of the death of Socrates—a memorable piece of historical literature.

However mistaken they suppose Him to have been, the story of the man who was crucified for the love of men and for His hope for them will remind them of some things too easily forgotten—of the deep tragedy of human life, of the wrongs that may be done by people who are not especially bad through lack of thought and sympathy, and, above all, that there are levels of human goodness and heroism far above those on which we habitually live.

Like all other great and good men, Jesus puts us to shame, and we feel that in spite of all our cleverness and knowledge we are lesser men.

Most of these reflections will also be open to the Christian believer, though they will be transformed by his faith. The transformation arises from one fundamental belief expressed by St Paul in the words 'God was in Christ, reconciling the world to Himself'.

The atrocious agony and death of Jesus was an act of God, through which He reveals Himself as Love. By an audacious act of faith in Christ's Resurrection the tragedy has been turned into a 'divine comedy' and an event which, taken by itself, looks like an outstanding example of the problem of evil and one more proof that there is neither justice nor love in the constitution of the world, is recognized as the supreme revelation of divine justice and love.

Some Christian thinkers (Kierkegaard is the well-known example) have held that this faith is reached only through despair. A man looks the facts of existence and of his own existence, in the face, and finds no foundation for hope in them. When he has confronted the world without God honestly, out of his despair he reaches out his hand in the dark to seek the hand of Christ.

There is truth in this; man's need is the spring of faith, and until we are aware of the need, we shall not know the meaning of faith in its full dimensions. But I do not think that despair is the necessary prelude to faith, nor that faith is an irrational leap in the dark.

The world, and our situation in it, is not only evil and menacing: there are gleams of goodness and beauty, and, if cruelty and suffering abound, loving-kindness and wisdom abound too.

We are met by a dilemma; which of the two aspects of existence is the more significant, and which speaks to us more clearly of the being of God? We cannot prove either possibility and here the venture of faith comes in.

We trust that the gleams of justice, mercy and truth are surer guides to the answer to the riddle than the cosmic forces or the average animal behaviour.

So when we are asked to believe that God was in Christ on the cross, we have indeed to overcome doubts and difficulties and make a decision which can never be free from tension. But it is not a defiance of fact and reason. It is faith, but a rational faith.

Two thoughts for this Holy Week emerge: Can we live without this faith? Are we living in it?

Tuesday in Holy Week

VICARIOUS PUNISHMENT

One aspect of the atonement as understood by the Church is that Christ bore the due penalty for the sins of the whole world.

The conception of vicarious punishment is to be found in the New Testament and has entered deeply into Christian devotion, but to many today it seems both unreasonable and unjust.

What civilized judge would admit the possibility of a man undergoing a punishment for someone else's crime and allowing the culprit to go free? Stated baldly and in terms of ordinary human conditions the notion is preposterous. To get the idea, however, into proper focus we have to look at it in the light of two presuppositions which many of us do not make.

We have first to take seriously the belief that there is a divinely-established moral order which, owing to human sin, is realized only imperfectly. It follows from this principle that the purpose of punishment is not simply to protect society from criminals, and, if possible, to reform them, but to vindicate the moral order.

Now it is contrary to that order that the wicked should prosper at the expense of the innocent, and one of the purposes of any system of law should be to see that, so far as human wisdom can effect it, honest men should live in peace, while the unscrupulous and selfish individuals should suffer.

If we think, in our human way, of God as holy and just, we are committed to the belief that He is the moral governor of the universe and the sustainer of the moral law.

This does not conflict with the belief that He is love, nor does the lawful infliction of punishment where it is deserved contradict the command to love our neighbour because the collapse of the moral order would be the direst calamity which could befall mankind—including the criminals. Thus, to imagine that God must 'let everyone off', because He is love, is to forget His Holiness.

The second presupposition is that what the New Testament says about the possibility of identification of Christ with sinners, He being in them and they in Him, is not mystical metaphor but the description of a spiritual reality.

With these presuppositions in our mind, let us reconsider the doctrine of the atonement, as the release from guilt and punishment. Christ the Son of God, the Second Person of the Holy Trinity, in sheer love and compassion for sinners, wills to identify Himself with them and to take them into Himself as a part of His experience.

He is not only the representative of sinful humanity: by His own will He includes them in Himself with all their evil deeds and sinful imaginings. St Paul boldly says that 'He was made to be sin for us'. Only one who was without sin Himself could bear the penalty of all the sins of the world: He knew them. He experienced them in their full horror, while having no part in them.

This divine act of love is the atonement for the sins of the whole world. All are forgiven for Christ's sake. But we have to claim our forgiveness and respond to the self-giving of the Saviour, with our own self-giving to Him. In so far as the identification of myself with Christ is real, and I live in Him, I can pray with confidence in the words of the hymn,

> Look, Father, look on his anointed face,
> And only look on us as found in Him.

Thus we may represent to ourselves this great matter, but let us not think we have 'explained' it; mystery remains—the mystery of love.

Wednesday in Holy Week

The last days of Jesus' early life were crowded with events and it is not easy to reconstruct from the Gospels their precise order of occurrence. Clearly enough, however, they began with His entry from the Mount of Olives into Jerusalem amid the acclamations of His disciples, and they ended with His death on the cross amid the mockery and execrations of the populace, His disciples having forsaken Him and fled.

The reasons for this rapid change from exaltation to humiliation are an interesting subject for inquiry, but in Holy Week it will be more profitable for us to meditate simply on the facts.

On the day of the entry the inner circle of His followers hailed Him as King, remembering the prophecy, 'Behold thy King cometh unto thee, meek and sitting upon an ass'— a gentle monarch—while the general public regarded Him with curiosity and expectation as 'the prophet from Nazareth'.

The Evangelists would have us believe, with them, that both these opinions about Jesus were true and were vindicated by the course of events, but that they were not true in the sense in which either the disciples or the populace believed them. He was indeed a prophet speaking the word of God, but He did not presage the restoration of the Jewish national independence, and He was indeed a King, but His Kingdom was not of this world.

Now that the New English New Testament is available we can read the old story of the Passion in fresh words—in contemporary words—and no veil of archaic language stands between us and the narratives. We can read them as if the events they record happened yesterday.

For many this will mean that, as never before, the death of Jesus and its circumstances are apprehended as events that really happened to real persons. And probably the challenge of the story and the deep questions which it suggests will be sharpened in their impact.

We may read the story as one of merely human significance, thinking of the Crucified as just another well-meaning and unfortunate man. Regarded in this light it is the greatest of the world's tragedies, not a poetic creation but one acted out and suffered in real life. Even so, it will have its spiritual effect leaving us somewhat different through having taken it into our imagination. The pathos of a great man dying for a noble dream can move us to regret and shame for our normal commonplace and selfish lives.

But those who have told us the story, the Evangelists, did not read it so. To them what they recorded was not human tragedy but divine triumph. In the suffering and evil which was concentrated in Calvary they read the message that God is love and in His Son has come to the rescue of fallen and miserable mankind.

The King who reigns from the cross is not a person who acted out His life a long time ago, and then finished. He is alive for evermore and, as He promised, drawing men to Himself by the appeal of His sacrifice. The question we have to ask is: Were the Evangelists right, and if so, where do we stand in relation to the Crucified?

Maundy Thursday

The last chapter of the Epistle to the Hebrews includes a vivid sentence the meaning of which is not immediately obvious. The writer urges his readers, who were Jewish Christians, as follows: 'Let us then go to him [i.e., Jesus] outside the camp, bearing the stigma that he bore' (Hebrews 13:13). He is, in fact, asking them to become 'outsiders' as their Master was. Jesus was crucified 'outside the camp', that is the Holy City, as a symbol of His utter rejection by Church and people.

The recipients of the letter were in a moral dilemma. They were drawn by feelings of patriotism and loyalty to join with their compatriots in some dangerous crisis, but to do so would have meant forsaking Christ and His Church. The writer implores them to endure the reproach of being cowards or traitors and to hold fast their allegiance to Christ, the divine Outsider.

We do not know what effect the letter had, though its preservation suggests that some at least regarded it as an inspired word of God; even those who may have rejected its advice deserved sympathy, for it needs a wise and courageous man to judge rightly in a real conflict of loyalties. Indeed any sensible person will be reluctant to become an outsider. Apart from the inconveniences and emotional disturbance of the social outcast there are less personal reasons for shrinking from such a situation. The outsider, being opposed to the values approved by public opinion, loses the moral support which it gives to insiders. In his case the 'outer conscience', as it has been called, does not reinforce the 'inner conscience', but condemns it. One needs to be very sure of one's own moral judgement to endure this tension.

It would be absurd to regard all outsiders as heroes. For the most part they are nothing of the kind, but rather individuals with exaggerated egotism and a defective sense of social responsibility. But some are really heroic and are fighting valiantly for values which surpass those of the society which rejects them. No Christian could deliberately be an unconditional conformist. There must be a point at which we would rebel and, if need be, go into the wilderness to protest against evil.

But the Christian will never want to stay an outsider. He will remember that Jesus willed, and still wills, to be within every society and every heart; His lonely death was not a final despairing assertion of separateness from men: it was an expression of the love by which He purposed to 'draw all men unto Him'. And the Cross is the key by which He opens many doors into fellowship. If necessity constrains us, let us be strong enough to become outsiders, but always reluctant ones, and always hoping to return as insiders to bear our witness in the human community, which we must never hate or despise. We come back not as hidden enemies but as lovers misunderstood.

Good Friday

A SHOCKING EVENT

If we contemplate the Crucifixion in its stark superficial reality, ignoring the interpretations which faith has offered, it takes its place with innumerable other instances of innocence tortured and slain, of cruelty in high places and in crowds, and of the fanaticism which can grow out of sincere religion. We have in this incident, as it were, an epitome of many of the aspects of the world which make it hard to believe in the love of God. Where can we discern His presence in such a scene of suffering and triumphant infamy?

The reply of faith to this question is a startling paradox. God is present in the victim who is defeated and killed, the object of almost unanimous execration. This paradox, if we can believe it, is in fact, at least a partial answer to the problem of evil. It is an answer which will not satisfy the philosophers, for it presupposes a conception of Deity which looks like 'dualism'. We are led to think of God as involved in a cosmic conflict against evil in all its forms, and the idea is not far off, that the conflict is costly not only in human suffering but to God.

That suffering can enter into the divine experience is a suggestion from which Christian thinkers have often shrunk, and not without reason, for from our human point of view it seems that suffering implies limitation, so that the Eternal and Perfect God cannot suffer. Yet the New Testament revelation of God in Christ surely means that the

Second Person of the Holy Trinity, who is God, 'suffered for us men and for our salvation', and that His conflict and His agony are truly real—not parables or symbols or imagination, but actually existing experiences which have a significance for the lives of all of us.

This is closely related to the central belief of Christians that God is love, which is far more vital for us than the belief that He is infinite. If those attributes of God which A. N. Whitehead described as 'metaphysical compliments' contradict the love of God, they must be swept away, for they are not 'good news' but only interesting speculation.

But there is no need to sweep away these attributes hastily, for we have only an imperfect grasp of their meaning and implications, nor have we plumbed the depths of the statement 'God is love'. There is more to be learnt. What we need to guard is faith in the divine compassion against the desiccation of philosophical analysis, and for this purpose we must hold firmly the reality of the suffering of Jesus Christ, the only begotten Son of God.

Saturday in Holy Week

In the third chapter of St John's Gospel we are taken to the heart of the Christian faith with regard both to the revelation of God in Christ and to salvation through Him. All the Gospels bring out clearly that the Son of Man, for our redemption, suffered death and that His triumph over sin and death was manifested by the Resurrection. In St John's Gospel the apparent separation between the suffering of the Son and His glory is abolished and we are led to see that the Crucifixion was itself the entrance into glory; in short, that crucifixion and resurrection are phases of one saving act. Jesus compared His cross to the standard on which the brazen serpent was displayed, according to the narrative in Numbers, in order that the children of Israel might look on it and be healed. The Son of Man must be lifted up so that all may look on Him and, so He predicts, if He is lifted up He will draw all men unto Himself—and so unto God.

The spectacle of glory there offered to the world, we must note, is both one of unlimited human love which accepts death for the sake of 'friends' and also of divine love. For He who is lifted up is 'He that came down from heaven, even the Son of Man who is in heaven'. I do not know why the New English Bible translates these words as 'whose home is in heaven' suggesting that His sojourn on earth was an exile from heaven. I think that the hymn which says, 'The heavenly word, proceeding forth, yet leaving not the Father's side', is nearer to St John's meaning.

This is not a trivial point of merely academic interest, for it has a bearing on the whole interpretation of the Gospel. It is a writing of profound mystical insight, which is partly concealed under its apparent simplicity, and it regards the humiliation, the Crucifixion, the Resurrection and the 'lifting up' of the Son of Man not only as historical, or semi-historical, events but as symbols of eternal truths about the being of God. When Jesus says, 'He that has seen me has seen the Father', He means that the whole of His life and experience is a revelation of the Eternal God.

However this may be, there is a practical application of the gospel which is inescapable. The Christian is called to play his part in the lifting up of the Son of Man. When he was an unrepentant sinner he unwittingly contributed to the passion of Him who died for the sins of the world, and now that he is redeemed he cannot shrink from the task of making known the attractive power of the Crucified. Propaganda and doctrine have their obvious places in this campaign, but the most effective and indispensable means are that we who call ourselves Christian should show in our lives that the Son of Man has really drawn us to Himself and that He lives in us.

Easter Day

The first words of Scripture that many of us will hear on Easter day are those of the Epistle (Colossians 3:1–7), 'If ye be risen with Christ', which remind us that we are celebrating not only an event in the past, the Resurrection of Jesus, but the existence of a continuing risen life in which we share.

St Paul does not doubt that his readers are risen with Christ, for in their baptism they committed themselves to Him; the Apostle is concerned that they should remember and reflect upon the new life that is theirs. We have in these few verses a succinct statement of a fundamental idea in St Paul's teaching that, in the Christian experience, the death and rising again of Christ is reflected and reproduced. 'Ye are dead, and your life is hid with Christ in God'; the old self which conformed to 'the world' is defunct—that the new man in Christ may live.

As always with St Paul, this profound, and even mystical insight is immediately given a practical application. The question, What shall we do about it? is never far away in his Epistles. And here, in brief but pregnant words, he sums up the Christian's duty. The hope could be described as 'other-worldly', with qualifications. We are to 'set our affections' or 'aspire to' 'things above' where Christ is 'at the right-hand of God', and our expectation is not to be some earthly Utopia, but the 'manifestation of Christ' and a share in His 'glory'.

But the risen life does not have to wait for a 'far off divine event'; it can be lived, and must be lived, in this earthly life, though not in accordance with earthly motives and standards. The Christian is to be a representative and an example here and now of the life of the world to come. The Apostle describes it as 'hidden with Christ in God', by which he means, I think, that its ideals and values are incomprehensible to those who are wholly absorbed in the present world.

The Christian's duty follows from this. It is first negative; a renunciation of the impulses in his own nature which 'belong to the earth'. But the purpose is positive. By bringing our animal impulses under control and liberating us from the 'ruthless greed' which is a kind of idol worship the risen life makes room for itself to expand with us so that its positive and creative virtues may spring up bringing with them the peace of Christ. The end is not gloom but joy—'singing with grace in our hearts unto God'.

Who would deny, looking at the world as it is, that the gospel of the risen life meets real and urgent needs: and who, looking at himself, would not confess that he would be more human, happier and more at peace if he could remember every day the hope set before him and the power offered to him in Christ?

Low Sunday

<><><><><><><><><><><><><>✳<><><><><><><><><><><><><>

MAKE YOUR OWN CHOICE

The Epistle for Low Sunday (I John 5:4–12) brings to our notice a remarkable characteristic of St John's thought—his habit of thinking in contrasts.

Light and darkness, the world and the fellowship of Christian believers, life and death are among the most important pairs of opposites which run through his teaching.

This presentation of the Gospel as offering us a choice of either one of two alternatives is effective in conveying a sense of urgency and of the need for decision, but occasionally it leads to questions which, as I know from correspondence, trouble the minds of earnest enquirers. An example occurs in the Epistle: 'He that hath the Son hath life, and He that hath not the Son hath not life'.

The perplexity which some feel about this text arises from the fact that we have become aware of the existence of truly holy persons of other religions and of men who lived before the birth of Christ who showed that they possessed qualities which we associate with 'eternal life'.

The problem is: can we be content to believe that no one outside the Christian Church can be 'saved' in the sense of attaining spiritual 'life'? Some of us have been indebted to the writings of saints and sages who certainly were not Christian, for illumination and inspiration, and we shrink from the conclusion that they were all condemned to spiritual 'death'.

We have to remember that St John was writing to and for the men of his time without having before him the knowledge of the religions of mankind which we now possess. He was confronting paganism in decay, which was a part of the 'world' to be overcome. It was necessary to bring home to his readers that they had to reject their ancestral superstitions and stand firmly on the side of Christ and the religion of the Spirit. For them it was a plain *either-or*.

I do not think we can know certainly what St John would have said about the problem that troubles us, but we have a clue to his answer in another chapter of the same Epistle: 'Beloved, let us love one another: for love is of God' (1 John 4:7). For him the test of true religion was not orthodoxy or devotional feelings, but whether or not it inspired love of our fellow-men, and he was quite sure that where this kind of love was shown in action there was Christ.

Might he not say then, that wherever love of this other-worldly kind exists, those who manifest it 'have the Son', even though they have never heard the name of Christ? But at the same time he would add, I think, that these unconscious Christians would be strengthened and confirmed in their way to eternal life by the revelation in Christ that God is love.

But what concerns us more nearly is the message which John gave to his readers for their guidance. We too live in a world which is largely pagan, with values which are at variance with those of Christ. We too confront an *either-or*, and only one of the alternatives is the road to eternal life.

Second Sunday after Easter

CHANGING SYMBOLS

The second Sunday after Easter is often called 'Good Shepherd's Sunday' because both the Epistle and the Gospel refer to this symbol of Christ, which, according to St John, was adopted by our Lord Himself (John 10:11ff.).

This question of the great New Testament symbols has recently come under discussion with regard to their meaning to modern men and it has been suggested that the Christian faith needs new symbols or at least some revision of its symbolical language.

We can see that some of them, for example those drawn from the ritual of sacrifice, do not make the direct impact on the modern imagination which they had when the Gospel was first proclaimed, but even those images which are readily intelligible have changed and do not mean precisely what they did.

The picture of the shepherd as we know him today is not the same as the shepherd of biblical times.

Even the fundamental image of the Heavenly Father is affected by the alteration of our social and economic conditions. The imagery of the Bible is drawn from a relatively simple agricultural and patriarchal community, in which the father and the family played a larger part than they do in modern civilized countries.

Much of the power and the responsibility of the father has been taken from him, and in consequence his normal relation with his children is quite different from what it was even in fairly recent times.

Who could imagine, for example, a child of Biblical times or even of the nineteenth century, calling his parents by their Christian names? The current usage, which presumably expresses a feeling of comradeship, may be admirable, but it certainly implies a new conception of fatherhood.

Cordelia, I suppose, represents Shakespeare's ideal of filial love:

> Good my lord,
> You have begot me, bred me, loved me. I
> Return those duties back as are right fit,
> Obey you, love you, and most honour you.

They would sound strange if ever King Lear were performed in modern dress. Yet I do not see how we can modify the symbol of the Fatherhood of God to bring it up to date. No one would feel that the religious value of the traditional language had been preserved if we brought in a reference to the Ministry of Education or the London Education Authority, much as many children owe to them.

There is, I think, a very important reason why most of the symbols of the New Testament cannot be replaced.

Any new symbols would have to be drawn from scientific sources or from the organization of scientific civilization. That is to say, they would be impersonal, and in a wide sense, mechanical. Some religious teachers have attempted to use electricity as an analogy or symbol of divine grace—with dubious results.

The essence of the religious view of the world is, however, that the impersonal and the mechanical aspects of reality are not the whole, or the central, truth. Deeper than they is the life of the Creative Spirit who is found in personal life and personal relations.

The great symbols of our faith remain. Unless we use our imaginations they may be dark to us, as indeed will be all the world's poetry. Do we ever pray that our imagination may be enlightened? We have need to.

Third Sunday after Easter

REVERSING THE VERDICT

When the Church started on its career one of its hardest tasks was to reverse a verdict and to do this in a most absolute way: not simply to show that the accused were wrongly condemned but that the accusers were the criminals.

In the eyes of those to whom the gospel was first preached Jesus was a dangerous transgressor who was justly punished and thereby righteousness vindicated. Their consciences were satisfied.

The Gospel for tomorrow (John 16:16ff.) reminds us that the gift of the Holy Spirit which Christ promised to His Church was intended to help it to persuade men to reverse this judgement and to convince them that the criminal who had been crucified was the supremely righteous one. Not only so, the tables were to be turned and the judges confounded by the assertion that the crucifixion of Jesus was the paradigm of all sin.

Light had come into the world and man preferred darkness. In this way the Holy Spirit would 'convict the world in respect of sin'. That this was the effect of the early preaching of Christianity we have evidence in the New Testament. Those who were moved at all by it were 'pricked at the heart'—an apt description of the sudden stab of suspicion that one has been utterly mistaken and has based one's life on a false assumption.

Conviction of sin has always been a primary element in

Christian experience and Christian preaching and it must always be so, for until the hard shell of self-complacency has been pierced we are deaf to its message. But it changes in the manner of its development.

There are very few today who would think of Jesus as a justly sentenced criminal, and probably most of those who know anything about Him would concur in reversing the verdict and agree with the Centurion that He was a righteous man and was judicially murdered.

But this historical opinion is very far from being a conviction of sin and we may hold it without any uncomfortable sensation of being pierced at the heart. We do not begin to approach that until we have the wish to reverse the verdict not only in our intellects but in ourselves and see ourselves as among the guilty.

Conviction of sin has been urged on many grounds, such as terror of divine judgement on failure to obey the law of God, and many are the devices by which we can ward off the indictment. We may, for example, argue endlessly on the question of guilt and how far we are really responsible for our actions or our characters.

The New Testament method, I think, is really more fundamental. It presents to us the truly righteous one, Jesus with His heroic virtue and His unlimited love, and it says to us, 'Here is goodness and innocence.' We do not have to debate the question whether this is true, for we know that in the presence of this man, we have indeed no cause for boasting. He towers above us, and compared with His purity of heart we say of ourselves, 'All our righteousness is as filthy rags' (Isaiah 64:6).

To be convicted of sin is then often the initial experience

of the Christian pilgrimage, but we need a similar conviction, though perhaps less shattering, as we pursue our way.

We stop and look at ourselves and look at Christ. Does not it sometimes seem that we have forgotten whom we serve? Self-complacency has seeped back and the standards of the world have resumed their sway over us. Miserable sinners that we are, have we really anything to boast of except that Christ still loves us?

Fourth Sunday after Easter

TELLING THE TRUTH

To tell the truth is no easy matter and to tell the whole truth about anything is almost impossible; nor is it quite simple to tell nothing but the truth, so readily do our imaginings mingle with our recollections. Yet morality agrees with religion in demanding truthfulness. To-morrow's Epistle and Gospel sound the note of truth. We are born again, writes St James, by the Word of Truth (James 1:17ff.) and St John records the Saviour's promise of the coming of the Spirit of Truth (John 16:5ff.). From the standpoint of rational ethics speaking the truth may be regarded as a part of the cardinal virtue of Justice. I owe it to my fellow-men that I should not deceive them in my words or conceal from them any truth which they have a right to know.

We may draw a distinction between lies and untruths. A lie is a false statement intended to mislead. Whether there can be situations in which a lie is justifiable, or even worthy of commendation, is a controversial question, but probably most of us would agree that in some circumstances the consequences of disclosing the truth could be so terrible that any plausible lie would be rightly preferred by a just man. A member of a resistance movement in a country occupied by enemies when under interrogation by his captors would, out of loyalty to his comrades, employ any deception to avoid betraying them. In such a case justice itself seems to require that the normal rule of truth-telling should be superseded. But fortunately practical dilemmas of this kind are not the stuff of which our everyday experience is made and lying remains in general both morally degrading and sinful. When we tell a lie we should feel that we have fallen below our best selves and have stained our souls in the sight of God.

All lies are untruths, but not all untruths are lies. We often say things which are not strictly true without any intention of deceiving our hearers or gaining advantage for ourselves. And this is largely because of the close association of memory with imagination, which is a common experience of all but the most matter-of-fact persons. We have a remarkable or amusing episode to narrate to our friends, and we find that it goes well. Such is human nature that we repeat it on appropriate occasions; we may even, as they say, 'dine out on it'; then, after an interval, we review the story and ask ourselves if it is quite the same as when we first told it. It is probably better, because our imagination has embellished and vivified it. Only a very stern moralist would condemn this as lying, and to do so would be to attack a considerable body of the wit and humour of human existence, but we must beware lest we insensibly overstep the line and, without being conscious of it, hope to deceive our hearers. Our hidden motive may be to present an unduly favourable image of ourselves, representing ourselves as cleverer or more magnanimous than we really are. We cannot go far wrong if our stories are always against ourselves—but this appears to be unusual!

Laughter which is 'of the truth' is a wonderful gift of God; the father of lies, we are told, is Satan—and I think he does not laugh.

Fifth Sunday after Easter

TRUE RELIGION

The nature of religion and the meaning of 'true religion' are questions much debated, and in the Epistle for tomorrow (James 1:22ff.) we may think we have found a biblical answer to them. 'To visit the fatherless and widows in their affliction and to keep himself unspotted from the world', we are told, is religion 'pure and undefiled'. From this some have deduced that conduct is the only important element in religion and everything else in it can safely be ignored. 'For creeds and laws let fools and bigots fight: He can't be wrong whose life is in the right.' The Greek word, however, translated 'religion' seems to be used normally for a particular aspect of religion—its outward expression, especially in public worship, and if we follow St James's argument it is clear that religion for him consists in 'hearing the word', remembering it and doing what it enjoins. Right conduct flows from attending to a divine message, understanding it and believing it.

We cannot quote St James as authorizing us to sweep away all doctrine and theology together with all study of liturgy and the modes of Christian worship. This does not imply that his dictum on pure religion has no relevance to Christian thought. We may take it as a warning that our thinking must never lose sight of the practical problems of Christian living in the world. Theology can be a fascinating study of questions, controversy and research—enough to absorb the interest and energy of a lifetime. I cannot but think that too often theologians would have done better if they had constantly borne in mind that the beliefs which they analysed were the stay and inspiration of millions of simple persons who were trying to follow Christ by loving their neighbours and preserving their integrity against the lower standards of the world around them.

Nor can we dismiss as negligible the inquiry by learned men into forms of Christian worship. The history of liturgies can help to bring us into contact with the experience and devotion of former generations, and it is no unworthy task to seek the words and acts which express most adequately the worship which we owe to God as revealed in Christ, but here most of all it can be fatal to forget the world which lives and struggles outside the Church. In this aspect of religion we can apply the test, 'by their fruits'. A technically perfect service may be deaf and dumb, if it has no power to move us to acts of love and purity of heart, while no doubt many a deplorable service, from the aesthetic and liturgical points of view, is blessed by God because it is understood by the hearts and minds of sinners who are endeavouring to be saints.

Ascension Day

The Christian Religion is the most 'historical' of all the great religions. Not only does it centre upon an historical Person, but its presentation of divine revelation is in the form of an historical development. The essential message of some religions can be distilled into statements of timeless truths or moral ideals, but in Christianity the history is part of the essence and its message most naturally comes to us as a long story in several chapters.

The Ascension of our Lord is the end of the central chapter. It marks the conclusion of the earthly life of the Redeemer, who is also the apex of revelation. According to St John, Jesus himself said that it was expedient He should go away in order that the Comforter might come (John 16:7); the Ascension was the final sentence in one chapter and the prelude to the next. And indeed all the chapters in the long story make a coherent whole so that we cannot fully understand them unless we perceive their relation with one another. The revelation in the historical Jesus, in His life and His teaching and in His death, leads backward to the Law and the Prophets and forward to the revelation of the Spirit in the Church. But not only do we need the previous chapter to understand; it actually lives on in the chapter which follows. Christ does not abolish the Law and the Prophets. They are the basis and the background of His life and thought; as He said, He did not come to destroy but to fulfil them.

As we now turn the page and pass on to the phase in revelation which comes next we should remember this continuity. The era of the Spirit, if we may use that term, is new. The Ascension is a real break, but it is not an absolute one, for the succeeding phase grows out of the mission of Christ and carries forward His revelation. The Spirit, He said, 'shall take of mine and show it unto you'.

Some have complained that the teaching of Christ as it has come down to us is fragmentary and not always clear. Why, they ask, did He not give explicit answers to many questions which perplex us? Such criticism is based on a misunderstanding. The process of revelation, though it culminated in Christ, did not end with the Jesus of history. Had He laid down final and detailed principles He would have confined the freedom of the Spirit. The present chapter, in which we have a part, is one in which the mind of Christ is applied by the Spirit to changing circumstances and demands.

But we must beware also of falling into the opposite error, that of leaving the revelation of 'the days of His flesh' behind as something now transcended. How can we know that what claims to be the inspiration of the Spirit is genuine? May it not be the utterance of misguided enthusiasm, or the merely human pronouncements of ecclesiastics? Always we must turn back to the central chapter in the story of revelation for our touchstone, asking whether what is proposed to us as the Spirit's leading bears the mark of the Redeemer.

Sunday after Ascension

CHARITY'S VEIL

At Ascension-Tide we are reminded of the continuing work of Christ for us. He has passed into the heavenly places to intercede for us and to plead His sacrifice of love as the charter of our redemption. 'Charity covers a multitude of sins', we read in the Epistle (I Peter 4:7–11): surely an appropriate reference to the divine charity which casts a veil, the veil of Christ's offering, over our offences.

The words have become a proverb, and it is likely that they were a proverb among Christians when the Apostle wrote his letter in which they occur. It may be that they are one of the sayings of Jesus not recorded in the Gospels. Like most other proverbs, this one is susceptible of more than one interpretation. Men have asked, whose charity and whose sins? I think if we read the beginning of the chapter we may conclude that the Apostle was referring chiefly to the original recipients of his letter. He mentions their conduct when they had been pagans, its debauchery and idolatry, contrasting it with their rule of life as Christians. It is natural that he should go on to write that these past sins were now obliterated and covered by their love of God and of their neighbours.

But this charity which was now their guiding principle became theirs through their faith in Christ. They loved, because God had first loved them, and their charity to others is a reflection of the Charity of Christ.

Can our charity cover the sins of others? A common

misunderstanding of this proverb may lead to serious error in practice. Some have supposed that the charity recommended to us means that we should cast a veil over their sins by pretending that they are not really sinful and cultivating an easy tolerance of relaxed standards, or an unfounded opinion that they are not really responsible for their actions. This is not the way of Christian charity: we shall do no good to our neighbours if we encourage them to persist in a mistaken estimate of their condition, and by complacency we may erode the authority of our own consciences. Nor can we repent for the sins of others. In this matter we are to imitate the Lord Jesus, who knew to the utmost the horror of sin, but loved to the utmost all the sinners. It may be, however, our privilege to share in the atoning work of Christ by unwavering charity and hope. We may try to see the good in the unrepentant sinner which waits to be released by the power of Christ, and we may pray for him. Often the loving patience of a friend, though it cannot weave the veil, has led a sinner to find for himself the charity which will cover his multitude of sins.

Whit Sunday

The Collect for Whit Sunday asks that by the aid of the Holy Spirit we may have a 'right judgement in all things' and through all the Christian centuries men have prayed for divine guidance in matters both of public and private concern. It must be owned that a survey of the decisions of synods and similar bodies which invoked the Holy Spirit is not altogether encouraging, for it is only too plain that in many cases the decisions were wrong and, further, that their assurance of the guidance of the Spirit has frequently made persons more obstinate in their folly. The need for some careful thinking on spiritual guidance is evident.

I do not think we can rule out of account the simple common-sense view that divine guidance may take the form of direct inspiration whereby the believer who prays is supernaturally given ideas and purposes. 'Intuition' is quite a common experience and thoughts and resolves seem to appear suddenly in the mind, as if coming from outside, not thought out but bestowed.

It is, of course, easy to be mistaken in our belief that our intuitions are given by God, but the belief itself is not absurd; if we hold that there is Eternal Mind in which we as minds live and have our being, it is actually probable that some of our intuitions are inspirations. But it would be un-Biblical to suppose that all divine guidance comes by inspiration similar to that of the prophets. The special grace of prophesy is not normal, nor is it promised to us. The normal guidance for which we may hope must be effected by means of our normal human faculties.

A pernicious error, which has side-tracked many well-meaning persons, is to imagine that when you have invoked the Holy Spirit as guide you have passed on all responsibility and can leave all the work to Him. An important principle of the theology of grace is that grace does not abolish nature, but purifies, refines, invigorates, and perfects it. And this somewhat abstract statement has practical applications. When I pray for divine guidance I shall not assume that it is beyond my understanding. I shall not allow my reason to fall into abeyance so that the Spirit may have scope; I shall pray rather that the Spirit will give my intelligence power and concentration on the matters of vital moment.

To live the life of the Spirit can be a wonderful medicine for a mind diseased or enervated, for, like a bracing wind, the Holy Spirit can clear my mind of irrelevancies, which divert its aim. While personal resentments, selfish ambition, pride or sensual imagination cloud my intelligence it cannot do its appointed work; a mind set free by the Holy Spirit is ready for the search for truth and apt to form right judgements.

Trinity Sunday

Some who think about the meaning of prayers put into their mouths by the Church may wonder what they ought to mean by the phrase in the Collect for Trinity Sunday, 'Keep us steadfast in this faith'. The words refer to the doctrine of the Trinity, a doctrine which has been the centre of much dispute, which is so recondite that Fathers of the Church have owned it was beyond their comprehension, and which, by its very nature, must be far short of the truth, for it would be foolish to imagine that the Being of God can be adequately expressed in human words and categories.

Is it reasonable, then, to pray that we should adhere rigidly to a belief which cannot be final? It seems evident that there is at least one prayer which must take precedence of that for orthodoxy—the prayer for truth. If I am, in the words of the Gospel, 'of the truth', I shall eagerly seek to know and embrace all the truth of which I am capable, and pre-eminently all the truth relating to my experience of God.

The Christian faith is a coherent body of doctrine and to worry about single doctrines in isolation is a waste of effort; I cannot keep looking over my shoulder or ask for proofs every time I say the Creed. So it is quite reasonable for me to accept the doctrine of the Trinity and the formulation of it which the Church offers so long as I am prepared to reconsider my assent if cogent reasons are forthcoming.

Two possibilities present themselves. It is theoretically conceivable that I might be persuaded by argument that the whole doctrine is radically wrong and based upon a misconception; in this case honesty would compel me to renounce it. But a far more likely situation is that I should be led to the conclusion that the doctrine is wrongly stated and needs to be formulated in terms which are more intelligible to modern minds. If that is my view, then I am fully justified in praying the words of the Collect, for an indispensable need in keeping myself and others in the faith of the Holy Trinity is that we should never cease to seek a deeper knowledge of God.

But however far we go in spiritual knowledge and understanding we shall never know God in the same sense as we know laws of nature or scientific truth. Not concept but symbol will be our mode of apprehension of the Eternal. Thus, though we may hope that here or hereafter we may have more light on the mystery of the Godhead, our knowledge will be expressed in the language of poetry rather than the language of science. After all, poetry rather than mathematics is the language of love.

◇◇◇◇◇◇◇◇◇◇◇◇◇◇◇◇◇◇—❋—◇◇◇◇◇◇◇◇◇◇◇◇◇◇◇◇◇◇

INVISIBLE REALITY

'No man hath seen God at any time', we hear in the Epistle for today (I John 4:7–21), and perhaps we remember that last Sunday, in the passage from Revelation appointed for the Epistle (Revelation 4:1–11), St John, 'in the Spirit', seems to assert that he saw God sitting on the throne in Heaven and proceeds to describe His appearance. At first sight, there appears to be a contradiction here, which is particularly remarkable if the tradition is right that both passages were written by the Apostle John. The apparent contradiction is, however, more verbal than real—it is indeed an illuminating paradox.

A fundamental principle of spiritual religion is that God is 'invisible', in the sense that nothing which we apprehend by sight or sound, and no creation of our imagination, can represent the being of the Eternal Godhead. He dwells 'in light unapproachable', and even 'light' is an inadequate symbol. Thus the spiritual life has to be expressed in a paradoxical form. The man of faith lives as one who 'sees Him who is invisible' and who knows that 'the things that are seen are temporal, but the things that are unseen are eternal'.

In our time the insight that the abiding and unchanging realities are invisible is particularly difficult to maintain because the whole emphasis of our civilization is on the world which we perceive and on the control of nature through discovery of its laws. The prevailing philosophy questions the assertion that there are realities inaccessible to our senses and, so far from agreeing that unseen and invisible things are the most real, would doubt whether they exist at all. Only by constant contemplation, in which we remind ourselves of our basic conviction that 'God is spirit', shall we be able to stem the tide of current thought and feeling.

A question is asked which must have an answer. If, it is said, God is, in this comprehensive meaning, invisible, how can we know anything about Him? And what do we mean when we say, 'I believe in God'? The short answer to this question is that, while we cannot even begin to understand the nature of God, there are symbols through which He reveals Himself. The Incarnation in Jesus Christ links the unseen with the seen, and things of time which pass away may be sacraments of the Reality which is eternal.

St John, we must observe, has a short and simple answer on which we could meditate without end, for he goes on to say, 'If we love one another God dwelleth in us and his love is perfected in us.' The whole Christian faith is in these words, which a child can understand, but a philosopher could not fathom. We find God in ourselves when we love one another. We cannot define Him; we do not have to. What we have to do is to recognize Him in every loving impulse of our hearts.

Second Sunday after Trinity

SURPRISED BY HATE

'Marvel not . . . if the world hate you': so the Epistle for today begins (1 John 3:13–24). Perhaps the words seem irrelevant to us, for normally today Christians do not arouse hatred by their faith, at least in our land—ridicule, indifference or contempt perhaps, but not active hate. Those to whom St John wrote understood very well what he meant, because they were reminded every day that they were a small minority trying to live on principles which were radically different from those of the society around them.

St John regards the hate of the world for the Christian brotherhood as the effect of an inevitable conflict. The Christian believer has his earthly home in the Church, in the fellowship of those who love one another, and in that experience they know that they have passed from death into life and are 'of the truth', that is in the realm of reality. Some difference of emphasis may be noticed, perhaps, between St John and St Paul in their dealing with the question of the relation between the Church and 'the world'; St Paul had to consider the practical day-to-day needs of his converts for guidance, but in essentials the two Apostles agree. Both recognize the conflict of values and both assert that the way of love is the way of truth and reality.

When this kind of fundamental conflict is taken as literal fact, it follows that God has enemies. 'The world' is at enmity with God, and its hatred may easily appear to deserve hatred in return. So indeed it has happened, for one of the most moving of the Psalms (139) expresses this feeling of one who trusted in God, 'Do not I hate them that hate Thee? Yea, I hate them right sore, even as though they were mine enemies.'

But this is not the attitude of the New Testament. It is no victory for love, but rather defeat, if our zeal for the Kingdom of God impels us to increase the hatred in the world. Hate cannot be overcome by hate, but only by patient love. It was a difficult assignment that St John, following his Master, gave to his spiritual children—to hate the world, in the sense of a way of life and a scale of values which were opposed to God, but at the same time to love those human beings who made up 'the world' and accepted its standards.

Though we are not in precisely the same circumstances as the Christians of the first century, the conflict is going on now and the world is still with us. God has enemies now as He had then. They are not so easily recognized and the issue is not so clear cut; it may even be that a 'fifth column' in the Church is one of the world's strategems. Are we quite sure which side we are on; and if we are on the Lord's side, are we fighting His battle with His weapons, not with hate but with love?

Third Sunday after Trinity

The word 'dialogue' has become familiar in connexion with political, social, and religious differences: we often hear that, somewhat to our surprise, we are involved as members of a church or a movement in a 'dialogue' and wonder what is happening. A dialogue, we may suppose, is intended to be different to an 'encounter', an argument, a controversy, a dispute, in this respect—that it is conceived as a step towards reconciliation.

When we profess to be conducting a 'dialogue' rather than a controversy we must mean that our aim is first of all to explain to those taking part in the dialogue our own point of view and to learn from it a fuller understanding and appreciation of theirs. But 'point of view' is not all. In dialogue, novelists and playwrights develop the characters of the persons in their story, and in real life we come to know our friends and companions by talking to them, nor can we be satisfied with mere talk, words which express the superficial aspects of our minds and theirs; the true fruits of dialogue can be reaped only when all engaged speak freely and sincerely out of their best thought and most significant experience. Dialogue should lead not to argumentative victory, and not only to intellectual synthesis, but to personal harmony of feeling and aspiration.

That 'dialogue' should be coming into favour in many fields of disagreement and controversy is a hopeful sign of the times and there is plenty of good will available, but perhaps the difficulty of sustaining fruitful dialogue is not sufficiently recognized. It is not easy to explore sympathetically views and sentiments which are quite contrary to those we hold sacred, nor to recognize that others when they enter into dialogue with us have similar feelings of repulsion.

At first sight, it is odd that 'dialogue' has originated as a conciliatory technique in religion and has had its chief success there. One might have thought that the tradition in Christianity of dogmatic orthodoxy, fortified by anathema, would have been too tough, but on reflection it is not really surprising, for all Christians believe in God and in revelation through Christ. They share at least two major presuppositions. And this may suggest to us a further question. For the believer all dialogue is in the presence of God, and in dialogues on Christian fellowship that presence is a consciously accepted and proclaimed fact; is there any sense in which we can reverently think of God as one of the interlocutors?

Fourth Sunday after Trinity

We may have dialogues with other men about God, and in consciousness of the presence of God, but can we without irreverence imagine a dialogue with God, one in which He is an interlocutor? Our children, when very young, do not shrink from telling us what they said to God, and what He said to them, but we, in our adult 'spirituality', have left such childish imaginations behind.

The idea, however, has a place in the Bible, and not only in passages which reflect primitive and crudely anthropomorphic images of deity. It occurs in places which are recognized as among the most 'spiritual' and 'inspired' in the Old Testament. These references to a dialogue with God fall into two classes—those which complain that dialogue had not been possible and those which give some account of interchange of thoughts with Deity.

The salient example of the first kind is the Book of Job. The audacity of this poem is often overlooked because its main purport is hidden from the reader by much rhetoric. Job has a grievance against God. He is convinced that no sins of his have deserved the misfortunes which he suffers and that his demand for justice meets with no reply from God. 'O that I knew where I might find him, that I might come even to his seat! I would order my cause before him and fill my mouth with arguments. I would know the words which he would answer me and understand what he would say unto me' (Job 23:3ff.).

The end of the Book of Job consists of a reply which is not an answer—the Lord's rejoinder 'out of the whirlwind'. It is important to notice that there is no attempt to meet the case which Job wanted to submit, no hint of any vindication of the justice of the distribution of pleasure and pain and good or evil fortune. The Lord's reply is an 'argumentum ad hominem', one which is based on the circumstances of an adversary. 'Who is this that darkeneth counsel by words without knowledge?' (Job 38:3ff.).

Then follows a magnificent poem on the wonders of the creation intended to awaken the awe of the reader and persuade him that the only thing to say about the problem which troubled Job is that the human mind cannot understand these questions and must bow in submission before the inscrutable majesty of God. When we turn to the other instances of dialogue between God and man we shall find a more encouraging suggestion.

Fifth Sunday after Trinity

According to Hebrew tradition Moses entered into dialogue with God. 'The Lord spoke unto Moses face to face as a man speaketh to his friend' (Exodus 33:11). To critical readers this text may appear good evidence of ancient Hebrew belief, but doubtful evidence for an actual human experience. Another narrative in the Old Testament, however, strikes us as almost certainly authentic in its account of dialogue between God and man—the case of the prophet Jeremiah (Jeremiah 1). The 'word of the Lord' opened the conversation with the statement that God had predestined and consecrated Jeremiah to be a prophet. Jeremiah was appalled at the announcement. 'Then said I, Ah Lord God, behold I cannot speak, for I am a child'; to which God replied: 'Don't say that, because I shall send you all the same, and you will deliver my message.'

The Lord touched his mouth, so the prophet thought, to signify that He had put His words into Jeremiah's mouth. The narrative proceeds to describe the two enigmatic 'signs' and their meaning. This passage, as it seems to me, gives us the best clue we have for a sympathetic understanding of what being a prophet involved. No doubt prophets varied in their experiences and no two were precisely alike, but the dialogue form was evidently a constant feature in the call and work of the prophets. It is not wide of the mark to imagine that, at the height of the prophet's obedience and response to the divine vocation, he felt that God spoke to him 'as a man speaks to his friend'.

In our previous study of the dialogue with God, we considered the case of Job, whose aspiration was some such encounter in which a revealing word would be spoken, but who received only overwhelming proof of the power and majesty of the Creator. Job was not a prophet, and it is surely significant in that he differed from the prophet in his aspiration and obedience. Job hoped for an experience which would solve his personal problems, vindicate his integrity, remove the sense of injustice under which he laboured and make him happy once more in his personal relation with God. A prophet like Jeremiah had another kind of aspiration, concern and obedience. He was anxious about the people of God, he thought of himself as one who was involved in the misfortunes, sins, and hopes of his brethren. It was Jeremiah who had the intelligible answer, because the question he asked was not how can I understand, but what can I do for my brethren and companions?

Perhaps another question suggests itself to us; all this talk about dialogue: who knows whether Job and Jeremiah were not just talking to themselves?

Sixth Sunday after Trinity

INNER DIALOGUE

Recent comments about 'dialogue' have called forth some interesting communications from persons who believe that they have heard a supernatural voice warning or encouraging them in moments of tension. It seems that Joan of Arc's 'voices' are not so exceptional as we may have imagined. Socrates, we remember, took great care to follow the direction of his 'daemon' and noted that its intervention was, in his case, always negative, advising against contemplated action. For what it is worth, my impression is that contemporary accounts of 'voices' would suggest for the most part, that they too urge, 'Refrain'.

There can be no doubt that these experiences are authentic, in the sense that voices are really heard and that they are heard as coming from outside—they are often located by the hearer as coming from a definite part of the room. I have never come across a case in which the 'supernatural' voice is heard by more than one person, and so far as I know, no one has ever claimed that a tape recording or any other mechanical recording has been made of such utterances. The facts, as they are known to us, are that 'voices' are heard by some persons which seem to have an authoritative message but originate neither from individuals other than the hearer, nor so far as he can tell, from the hearer himself.

We may perhaps venture to conjecture that all this can help clarify the inspiration and the call of the prophets.

When they announce that the 'word of the Lord' has come to them we must take them literally. They did have this experience of a supernatural voice speaking to them and they did recognize it as possessing an authority which brooked no question. They did not argue—they proclaimed. When St Paul had his conversion experience he too heard a 'supernatural' voice, the voice of the risen Christ, which halted him in his persecution of Christ's disciples and changed the whole course of his life. Though the accounts of Paul's conversion do not agree in every particular it is clear that his companion did not hear the voice; they did not at least get the message.

The human mind can be an instrument for the apprehension and the communication of the divine truth. That is the presupposition of all belief in inspiration and revelation. If we look closely at our own minds we may discover that we are engaged in an internal dialogue in which it is conceivable that God may intervene.

Seventh Sunday after Trinity

VOICE OF CONSCIENCE

Everyone would agree that we should attend to the voice of conscience, but comparatively few are able to give an account of what they mean by conscience. This is no wonder for great thinkers have differed seriously on this question.

Two explanatory titles have been much explored in the age-long discussion of ethics, one emphasizing the intellectual aspect of conscience and the other the emotional. 'The practical reason' was the famous name which the German Kant adopted, 'the moral sense' the epithet favoured by some English and Scottish philosophers.

The first of these underlines the judgement involved in the activity of conscience—judgement on ourselves, on others and on actions. St Paul seems to have taken this view of conscience, so at least we may conclude from his description of the moral condition of the pagans, who, though they have no law like the Jews, are their own law (Romans 10.4).

When conscience is called the moral 'sense' the word means very much what it means in 'the artistic sense' or 'sense of humour', or 'the sense of what is fitting'—it is a feeling and a response to different kinds of actions, speech and character.

This too is a familiar experience which is referred to often in the Bible. We respond impulsively to deeds of heroic virtue, of unselfishness and holiness with admiration and joy, while we shrink instinctively from cruel, selfish, and treacherous acts and individuals. We don't need to argue the matter.

As one of the English 'moral sense' philosophers wrote: 'When I see a nasty fellow I recognize that he is a nasty fellow, just as when I see an ugly fellow I know that he is ugly.' The passages in the Bible where this kind of conscience is at work are too numerous to mention. How frequently both in the Old and New Testaments sin is identified with repulsive dirtiness and the process of redemption with the washing off of filth, while the righteousness of saints is symbolized by spotless flesh and spotless white clothing!

Thus we may conclude that both these descriptive titles of conscience are valid in that they are based on real and essential aspects of the experience which we refer to when we claim to have listened to the voice of conscience. Perhaps it is not possible to conceive of a person who had moral judgement but no moral feeling or moral feeling without moral judgement, and even if such a freak were conceivable it would not be fully human.

We have still, however, to ask which of the two titles, moral reason and moral sense, is the fundamental one, or are they perhaps both independent?

Eighth Sunday after Trinity

THINKING AND FEELING

The question whether conscience is a kind of thinking or a kind of feeling may seem unimportant, for we should readily agree that only a being who both thinks and feels would be capable of moral choice. Yet I think there is importance in deciding which of the two is fundamental and to me it is evident that thinking, intellectual activity, judgement is the core of the experience which we call 'acting conscientiously'. And we have some words of St Paul on our side, when, writing of the offering of the self to God which he regards as the supreme duty, he adds, 'which is your reasonable service' (Romans 12:1). Many differ on this point; indeed the same man may have different opinions at different times. Sometimes what conscience demands appears irrational and to proceed from emotional imagining, but when we think this out we are loth to accept the conclusion that we are required to do what is unreasonable and inclined to accept as really obvious that what is truly rational is truly right. That does not mean, of course, that what I regard as rational is necessarily right, because I may have 'the conscience of an ass'; my mind may be confused, or my information may be erroneous; but it does mean that right reason adequately informed is the authority to which I must defer. It would be a very queer and alarming world if we had to believe that moral conduct was irrational.

At the same time, the 'pure intellect', if there is such a

thing in nature, would be helpless in moral action. The intellect divorced from imagination, would be inert and impotent. Moral action is action concerned with other persons. We can hardly conceive of conscience apart from a society of persons. If there could be a human being born and grown on a desert island would he have any moral ideas? Perhaps he might develop a sense of duty to himself and to God such as Robinson Crusoe had, but Crusoe brought these ideas with him; he had acquired them in the community where he was born. It seems most unlikely that he could have invented them himself. Without imagination, and the emotions which it arouses and enriches, we could have very little social life. By imagination we make real to ourselves the existence of other persons and their needs; by imagination we enter, to some extent, their lives. Without imagination we cannot love, because only through imagination can we have practical understanding.

God, we may say, reveals Himself to and through human thought and human imagination. It is through them that conscience speaks in our hearts. In this sense conscience is the voice of God.

Ninth Sunday after Trinity

CONVERSATION

Conversation is not quite the same thing as dialogue. Both words denote communication by speech but, while dialogue implies exchange of thoughts in a consecutive and purposeful way, 'conversation' is apt to be desultory and wandering. Irrelevant remarks spoil a dialogue but may add to the liveliness of a conversation. Reading the Authorized Version of the English Bible might lead us to think that it had much to say about conversation; the word, at least, occurs frequently, but this is misleading, for in the time of James I when the translation was made, 'conversation' meant general social behaviour with no special reference to talking. Indirectly, however, the New Testament has some important strictures on conversation in our modern sense. In one respect at least, Jesus agreed with Socrates; both insisted that words wrongly used could be causes of pernicious errors in thought and conduct. The judgement of God, we are told in the Gospels, is upon 'every idle word'. Socrates laboured to find the true definition of words like 'justice', 'courage' and 'piety' lest we should deceive ourselves; Jesus demanded responsibility in the use of words lest we should deceive others. Both would teach us that plainness of speech is a virtue and the seed of other virtues; neither admired rhetoric or thought that truth was improved by being dressed in ornamental clothes.

Conversation is concerned with truth. Through conversation we acquire a large part of the knowledge which we label 'personal' because it is about persons and peculiar to us as individual persons. If the participants in a conversation are indifferent to truth and malicious, it will be a means of propagating falsehood and illusion, a kind of poisoning of the well of society. One of the ends we have in view in conversing with friends is to come to know them better and to invite them to come closer to us in some area of our private world. There are moments, perhaps rare, when we let down the barriers, when we lay aside all pretence, and when we stifle criticism, seeking only fuller understanding; at such times, we touch the sacramental and spiritual aspect of conversation. For the most part conversation is not at this level; we remain behind our defences and project our favourite images of ourselves: but even in this inferior mode our conversation can be a solace and refreshment when seasoned by honesty and goodwill.

MORAL VARIETY

They say that there are many ways of doing wrong, but only one way of doing right, but though eminent moralists have made this assertion, it is possible to doubt its truth. Any considerable acquaintance with 'good persons' whether in actual experience or in reading, will lead to the conclusion that, far from there being any monotonous sameness in good actions, there is a remarkable variety, that in fact the differences between one individual and another are nowhere more obvious than when they are acting with love and goodwill. No doubt the impression of sameness in virtuous conduct is due to the fact that moral principles are usually stated in the form of laws and rules, and these most often in negative form. There is only one way of abstaining from action, and though stealing can have almost infinite variety, not stealing is incapable of any. It is, however, a well-recognized fact that the formulation of moral principles as negative rules is unsatisfactory and misleading and needs to be developed into positive statements and definite ideals. When this is done, we find that the negative rules are special cases of, or deductions from, positive principles and ideals. Whether these higher principles are many or one is a disputed point. St Paul seems to hold that love is the supreme and sufficient principle and indeed fulfilling 'all the law', but it can be argued that there are some virtues and duties, recognized as such by all good men, which cannot be regarded as special cases of love and must be brought under the heading of 'justice'.

I find it difficult to dispense with justice as a principle distinct from love, because it seems to me that occasions often arise when we have to choose between trying to be just and trying to act lovingly. Those who tell us that to be just is really to be loving, or contrarywise that to be loving is really to be just, may be right, but the formula, though probably orthodoxly Christian, is not helpful in practice. For our immediate point this question does not much matter. The important thing is that right actions are not negative but positive, actions aimed at an ideal—that of love or of justice. The response, then, if this is the real situation, may be determined to a large extent by the personal make-up and the circumstances of the individual. The loving act, for example, of a plain, blunt man, will not be the same as that of a sensitive and imaginative woman, nor that of a millionaire as that of an old age pensioner. The rich variety of goodness may offer us an object worthy of our contemplation.

Eleventh Sunday after Trinity

◇◇◇◇◇◇◇◇◇◇◇◇◇◇◇◇◇❋◇◇◇◇◇◇◇◇◇◇◇◇◇◇◇◇◇

NOT SELF MADE

The 'self-made man' is not, I think, so frequently met either in real life or in fiction as he used to be. I suppose that since Victorian times, when he was a well-known character, we have all become somewhat more cautious in attributing any success which we may have had to our own abilities and virtues and somewhat more percipient of the part that circumstances have played in our triumphs. When we ask ourselves, 'what hast thou that thou did'st not receive?' we have to admit that, when we have eliminated our inherited qualities and the environment into which we were born, we may be left with a sadly diminished list of legitimate subjects for self-congratulation. Possibly they may have shrunk to a single item—well, I did not miss the opportunities that came my way.

In today's Epistle St Paul is led to give an account of his gospel, his career and his personality. He certainly is not inclined to call himself a self-made man, but he has a word to describe his development—'by the grace of God I am what I am'; he is a grace-made man. He attributes his outstanding and prosperous labours to the grace of God which has been with him. We must not imagine that he thought of grace in an impersonal way as though it were a force which acted in a mechanical or magical manner. That may have been the mistake of some Christians in later times, but for St Paul the word still has its original meaning of 'favour', loving-kindness directed towards an individual in need. If we would understand him, we must never distinguish between grace and the Holy Spirit or forget that it arises from the relation between human persons and the personal God.

When we bear this in mind we have already gone some way towards overcoming a dilemma which has troubled many. The question arises, Does not grace, and our dependence on it, supersede or abolish free will? But if grace is the loving relation between the personal God and a human creature we cannot believe that God wills to take away the quality in His creature which is the essential element in personality. What loving father would wish to turn his child into a puppet, however efficient?

'His grace was not in vain,' says St Paul. He had not missed his opportunities, and that was the only claim he had for approval. He had opened his heart to the love of God.

Grace comes to us too often in vain. We do not recognize it, or we do not ask for it, or we do not trust it, or we think that we can be 'self-made' men, but it is available and sufficient for every need. So at least St Paul believed, and it carried him through some rough places which would have daunted any self-made person.

Twelfth Sunday after Trinity

MORAL ATTITUDES

That there is a close connexion between morality and religion would be generally accepted, at least in Christian circles, and many would be inclined to put forward as one of the principal merits of religion that 'it makes people good'. But the matter is not so simple as we might suppose and the poet's identification of true religion with moral goodness, 'He can't be wrong whose life is in the right', will not stand up to the test of experience. The contemplation of one upright man who holds evidently mistaken beliefs (and they abound) is enough to refute it.

Of course it is difficult to find persons who are religious but not moral, or who are moral but have no vestige of religious feeling, but it is possible to distinguish between the religious attitude and the moral. The two attitudes of mind are symbolized in two attitudes of body. The man who is making a heroic moral decision stands upright, asserting his personal integrity in the face of opposition; the man who is reaching a religious crisis is on his knees, confessing that he has in himself no power to do anything that is good and must rely on God.

It is not surprising then that from both sides we have declaration of independence; some thoughtful believers refuse to take much account of moralists, and moralists declare that religion has nothing to contribute to the study of ethics. Though not surprising, however, it is deplorable, for though morals and religion are not identical, each needs the other. The danger for religion in disregarding ethical thought is that its understanding of human goodness and duty may become narrow and fanatical. 'New occasions teach new duties' and the conditions of life change; in our days very rapidly. The nature of the new duties cannot be known without reflection on the new situation and the possibility of enlarging, or modifying, the application of accepted principles. The 'public image' of religious persons as good people living in the past is no doubt unjust, but it is given a certain colour by Christians who quite rightly proclaim that the Christian faith can guide us in every case where moral decisions have to be made but do not attempt to show how this guidance works out in contemporary and unprecedented circumstances.

The moralist is often even less willing to listen to religion largely because he does not admit that the problem with which religion is concerned is his business. That problem is how to become good. The analysis of moral ideas, and all the rest of the fascinating inquiries of writers on ethics, one would think could hardly fail to pose the question, How is a good man produced? Here religion claims to be heard—and it is heard in St Paul's words in the Epistle for today; 'Not that we are sufficient of ourselves to think anything as of ourselves; but our sufficiency is of God' (2 Corinthians 3:4).

DEFINING THE GOOD

Ever since men began to think they have been discussing the meaning of the word 'good', and those argumentative types, the philosophers, have fiercely differed on the question whether there is a Supreme Good which includes all the lesser good things and, if so, what it is. To run through all the answers to these questions would entail an intensive course in the history of philosophy. Let us note one or two which have had many advocates.

An obvious one is that pleasure is the good and pain the evil opposite. Everyone, it is said, recognizes that pain is to be avoided and pleasure sought. These feelings, as it were, are built into our nature and we need no further reason. We can hardly deny the force of this, and I think we should agree that pleasure is, in some sense, good. But surely pleasure cannot be the whole meaning, for we should all condemn some pleasures as evil, **nor** do we admire as a good man one who devotes his whole energies to pleasure. To 'make a god' of pleasure, as we say, is not a term of approval. There must be, it would seem, some higher good, or innocent pleasures and those that are evil.

'Fulfilment' may stand for another kind of answer which has been brilliantly restated by Professor Brand Blanchard. It is that the good for each and every person consists in the development in a harmonious manner of all his potentialities so that he is all that he could have been. This answer has the merit of giving due place to pleasure while not enthroning it as the supreme good, for the realization of the powers latent in the self without discord must give rise to the purest and most lasting happiness. Of course those who hold this view would own that their ideal is unattainable in its completeness by any human being. Life is not long enough, and its limitations prevent our perfect fulfilment, but we can aim at an approximation to it, and to do so is to be, in intention, a good man.

Evidently this theory has hold of some part of the truth, but we may doubt whether it is the whole truth. Do we really want everyone to express all his potentialities? Do we even want to express all our own? And should we wholly approve of a man who concentrated on his own harmonious development? We might, I think, be inclined to complain that he was 'making a god' of himself.

The Collect for today speaks of so faithfully serving God in this life that we fail not to attain His heavenly promises. The Christian faith has a distinctive view on the definition of the good.

THE RELIGIOUS GOOD

Some important attempts to 'define the good' have been made by thinkers who approached the question without reference to religion. Two at least of them had seized part of the truth but were not wholly satisfactory. Can we find perhaps a better answer if we take religion into account and hear what it has to say on the Good?

There are several religions which could claim to be considered but in one important respect they agree as against the 'secular' moralists—on the nature of man. They would be at one in objecting that we are bound to go wrong in defining the good for man if we start with the assumption that he is nothing but an intelligent animal conditioned by time and space, and they would agree too that he is also spiritual by nature. Religion, in short, brings in a new dimension, insisting that the Good is that which fulfils man's spiritual nature.

The Christian religion, as we meet it in the New Testament, has many phrases to describe the Good for man—holiness, to know God, to see God, to be in Heaven. We could not say that all these expressions have precisely the same meaning, but fundamentally they spring from the same idea—that man's supreme good consists in being in harmony with God. The conception of harmonious relations appears in many theories about the Good, most clearly in that which bases itself on some kind of personal fulfilment; the religious definition takes this idea into its new dimension. It is not enough to be in harmonious relation with one's own potentialities and with our visible environment including other persons. In God 'we live and move and have our being'. He is our unseen, but most real, environment. Our highest good, and our most abiding fulfilment, would be to become at one with Him.

The Religious answer to the question, What is man and what is his true Good? assumes that man, as he stands, is incomplete and that this incompleteness cannot be overcome by any evolution or development in the future. It can be overcome, however, at least in part, by the turning of the human spirit to the Eternal Spirit, recognizing its own imperfections and the power of the grace of God to transcend them. Fulfilment means to be made whole in God.

But, we might object, does not this entail an otherworldliness which would so fix our hopes on the unseen and eternal that the good things of this world, yes, even the companionship of loved fellow creatures, would lose their values for us? That is a question which demands a reply.

Fifteenth Sunday after Trinity

THE GRATEFUL LEPER

Anyone who is doubtful about the reality of progress might reflect upon the plight of the ten men mentioned in last Sunday's Gospel (Luke 17:11–19). They were lepers who appealed to Jesus for help as He passed through Samaria; there was no one else they could appeal to, for their disease made them objects of fear and disgust and excluded them from human society. Leprosy was believed to be a special sign of the displeasure of God and a punishment for sin. This is still the case in parts of the world and for this reason the word 'leprosy' is not used by official bodies such as the World Health Organization. It is somewhat surprising that Jesus appears to have had free contact with lepers and to have included the 'cleansing' of lepers among the principal works of mercy which He and His disciples did, manifesting thereby the presence of the Kingdom of God.

In this respect it would seem that Jesus was at variance with the customs, and even the laws, of his nation. And this difference was based upon a difference in the conception of the relation of God to disease. The Jews, on the authority of some passages of the Old Testament, believed that leprosy was a visitation of God and a retribution for sin; thus even if they had known how to help lepers, it would have been of doubtful propriety to attempt to alleviate suffering ordained by Providence. Jesus, one must conclude, did not share this belief. He did not think of the

Father in Heaven in these terms. His conviction was that disease was caused by 'evil spirits', by powers opposed to God, and that 'the finger of God' could be seen not in the incidence of disease, but in the healing power which overcame it.

Leprosy is not yet banished from the earth. Dr S. G. Browne, a leading authority, estimates that there are at least ten million lepers in the world today, but they are not hopeless outcasts. Cure is not impossible and alleviation can be brought to those for whom recovery is not feasible. Research and organized help go forward. Dr Browne himself is a Christian medical missionary, and much of all the work in connexion with leprosy has been inspired by the example of Christ. May we not see in this a fulfilment of the promise of the Lord, 'Greater works than these shall ye do'? Without scientific knowledge and skill of medical experts they could not have been done, and without the dissipation of unworthy ideas of God and the compassion learnt from Christ they would not have been done. Science and Christian faith may sometimes be uneasy companions, but they must never be thought of as enemies of one another; through their co-operation real progress can be achieved and many lepers and innumerable other afflicted human beings have reason to be grateful.

Sixteenth Sunday after Trinity

<><><><><><><><><><><><><>—❋—<><><><><><><><><><><><><>

DEATH OF THE SELF

To one who skims the New Testament for the first time it may well seem that there is a contradiction in the Gospel as it affects our personal lives. On the one hand we are told that we need salvation of our souls and should be deeply concerned about them; but on the other hand, we read, 'Whosoever would save his soul shall lose it' (Mark 8:35) and even, 'He that loveth his soul loseth it, and he that hateth his soul in this world shall keep it unto life eternal' (John 12:25). How, we may ask, can we have this love-hate attitude to ourselves? Is it not a psychological impossibility?

We can discriminate between two 'selves', distinguishing the central and fundamental self from the self which is active in the passing concerns of every day—the individual who has a history and, after some years of varied experience, will die—'the soul in this world'. With this distinction in mind, we can see that the paradoxical teaching about saving our souls by not wanting to save them is neither contradictory nor impossible.

The New Testament, in agreement with much spiritual insight in other religions, asserts that we are subject to a dangerous illusion about ourselves, which consists in taking the ordinary self of day-by-day existence as the whole self, the only real soul we have. While under the influence of this illusion we are apt to imagine that the values, appetites, ambitions, hopes and fears of the lower self are what will satisfy us. We grasp at the objects which we suppose will fulfil our desires and enhance our personalities. Jesus described one type of this mistaken seeker for happiness when He said, 'A man's life does not consist in the abundance of the things he possesses.'

One of the tremendous truisms, accepted by cynics as well as saints, is that satisfaction and happiness on this level always elude us. 'There is not any hour complete, nor any season satisfied.' The cynic notes the fact with a wry smile, but the saint draws a conclusion. We have been looking too low for our happiness because we have misunderstood our own nature. We are, as Spinoza remarked, 'greater than we knew'. At the centre of ourselves we are immortal spirits in contact with God. So long as we fail to recognize this we shall miss our true life.

The death of the self is the necessary condition of the salvation of the self. We must break through the barrier of illusion that we may begin to know 'life that is life indeed'.

Seventeenth Sunday after Trinity

LUCK AND GRACE

'We pray thee that thy grace may always prevent and follow us': the words of the Collect may lead some who can look back over many years to ask themselves whether they can affirm that the grace of God has indeed been before and after in their experience. Any such retrospect must be coloured by the point of view from which it is made. We may recall what seem to be bits of luck, happy chances which turned to our advantage, offset by other occasions when, as we say, fortune was against us. We may dwell with satisfaction on our success in overcoming difficulties by clever management and with regret on our failures to cope with them. But these are not inquiries into the incidence of grace. To answer our question we have to ask: Can we discern in our experience a series of opportunities to serve our fellow men, to grow in spiritual understanding and in faith and love; and further, can we say from our experience that when hard decisions had to be made we were given the needed strength and courage? With this presupposition in mind our past lives take on a different aspect. Some of those strokes of luck do not look so admirable and perhaps too some of the misfortunes appear now to have been challenges to our manhood by meeting with which we were able to rise above ourselves and acquire, as it were, a new dimension. The days of struggle, no less than the days of calm, may be days of grace.

To ponder exclusively on the past is dangerous and un-

Christian. We are wrong to torment ourselves with recollections of sins which have been forgiven or to reproach ourselves with lost opportunities. Our concern is with the present and the future and the opportunities which remain. Yet to look back with a sincere desire to understand can itself be a means of grace. We can see now where we went wrong. No doubt we went wrong in many ways: through thoughtlessness, through selfishness, through fear, through ambition, through passion—through all the many sources of temptation which are common to humanity—but the root cause was that we lost hold on our faith in the meaning and purpose of our lives and in the reality and power of the grace of God. Our Christian forefathers spoke more often than we do about 'being in a state of grace.' Perhaps they often interpreted it too narrowly, but they had a grasp of an essential truth of religion. The sufficiency of grace was the anchor of St Paul's spiritual life; the word which came to him, 'My grace is sufficient for thee', carried him through all the tempests of his pilgrimage. So it should be for us. God's grace does 'prevent and follow us' and we may judge whether we are living in grace by the test suggested in this same Collect—if we are 'continually given to all good works'.

Eighteenth Sunday after Trinity

<>✦<>

DEMONIC DEVIL

The Collect for today refers to 'the temptations of the world, the flesh, and the devil'. The flesh and the world tempt us through our appetites, our vanity and our love of comfort and though they are often subtle or obscure, in a general way we know from experience what they are. But what are the temptations of the devil?

Whether or not there is a personal devil is really irrelevant, for whatever their source may be we can distinguish a class of temptations to evil which are unlike those of the world and the flesh. Whereas they appeal to what we call our 'lower nature' these have their target in our 'higher nature'—they arise because we are spiritual beings who are self-conscious and can set before ourselves ideals which we may pursue with steady and rational purpose. To fall a victim to the temptations of the devil means to pervert the very centre of our being and allow our spirits to become servants of destructive causes.

The essence of demonic evil is egoism swollen to an overwhelming pride. Those who are thus obsessed are not usually licentious or, in the ordinary sense, 'worldly'. Often they have many of the minor virtues and are able 'to scorn delights and live laborious days'—for their own ends. And those ends are the aggrandisement of the ego—power is the master motive, power not for the sake of any good that they hope to achieve for the world, but for its own sake.

The devil, we are told, revolted against God and tried to

make himself God. This is at least a parable of the progress of this obsession. When it touches the borders of madness the victim begins to regard himself as a deity. All is right that ministers to his self-assertion; he is the determiner of moral values; the conventions, the scruples, and the ethical judgements of his fellow mortals must give way before his superior claims.

Some of the 'great men' of history have been of this type, and it would be folly to suppose that the 'great men' of our own time are exempt from the temptation to demonic evil. Changes in the social and political order do not alter human nature fundamentally and the weakening of belief in God has probably made the danger more acute, for the atheist great man can feel no horror at the idea that he is putting himself in the place of God.

But we do not have to be 'great men' to experience the temptations of the devil. We are all inclined to 'believe in ourselves', which is surely the most unfounded creed ever devised, and to regard ourselves as the centre of the universe. The lust for power can devastate not only the whole world, but every little corner of it.

The remedy is a firm and rational belief in God, which will put us in our right proportions. It is quite a good little prayer: 'Grant thy people grace to withstand the temptations of the world, the flesh, and the devil, and with pure hearts and minds to follow thee the only God.'

Nineteenth Sunday after Trinity

CHRISTIAN ANGER

The world of the first century, like that of any other century, was full of antagonisms, grudges and resentments, but St Paul was determined that his Christian communities should be different from the world in this respect. He recognizes that anger is an instinctive reaction which cannot be wholly repressed. 'Be ye angry and sin not', he writes, and goes on to explain how that can be done. 'Don't let the sun go down on your wrath'—let it be a passing emotion; do not dwell on your wrongs or nurse your anger (Ephesians 4:26).

We read in St Mark that Jesus was angry, and at first sight there seems to be a contradiction between St Paul's advice and his Master's example. Jesus 'looked round with anger' on His critics in the Synagogue who were watching to see whether He would heal a man with a withered hand on the Sabbath day (Mark 3).

He was angry at the stupid fanaticism which would prevent Him from doing a work of mercy on the Lord's Day. Certainly the sun went down on His anger, for it was his constant attitude. The scribes and Pharisees who condemned His Sabbath-breaking may well have thought of Him as an 'angry young man'.

But we must note the cause of His anger. It was not any insult or injury to Himself which called it forth; it was the wrong done to His Father's name by the false idea of the divine nature which lay behind the opposition and the lack of sympathy with suffering and poor fellow men.

There is no real contradiction between the Apostle and the Lord Jesus. The former was dealing with private and personal resentments, the latter with public and far-reaching injustice, which would go on long after the day's end and be a burden for many tomorrows.

We need to discriminate between different kinds of anger. The kind of which St Paul writes, the smouldering grudge on which our memory lingers, is slow poison in the soul which, for our own spiritual and mental health, we must overcome by the will to forgive. The anger of Jesus, in so far as we can share it, must not be dismissed. Indignation at injustice and oppression is a mark of a sound and lively conscience. We may be deficient in this unselfish anger, too indifferent to the wrongs which others endure, too easily persuaded that nothing can be done, or persuaded by specious excuses.

There is, however, a word in the account of Christ's anger which cannot be overlooked. He was 'grieved at the hardening of their heart'. His anger did not lead to hate. He sorrowed not only for the wrong that was done, but for the misguided and perverted spirit of those who did it. If our anger is Christian, we must follow Christ in this: He loved and prayed for those with whom He was justly angry.

Twentieth Sunday after Trinity

TWO GREAT WORDS

Surely there is no more honourable title than 'Justice of the Peace' which brings together two great words and two noble ideals and suggests that they are intimately connected. Those who hold this title have the function of preserving the Queen's peace by administering justice. If I were asked for a motto for those who bear the title I could not think of a better one than a verse of the Psalms, 'Mercy and truth are met together; justice and peace have kissed each other' (Psalm 85:10).

The writer had a vision of a perfect society, or at least of one far better than any he had known in his experience, and he sees clearly that two kinds of virtue are needed for such a happy social order—the intellectual and the emotional virtues perhaps we may call them; there must be respect for truth and reality and the reasonableness which seeks justice, and there must also be that sensitiveness of feeling which produces sympathy and neighbourly affection.

Today's Epistle opens with the words, 'See that ye walk circumspectly, not as fools but as wise redeeming the time, because the days are evil.' I think St Paul's Greek means simply 'look carefully', or 'take careful heed', and the English translation 'circumspectly' introduces a slightly different idea. But certainly a most relevant one, for 'circumspectly' means, of course, looking round to see where you are, taking in the actual situation—and what could be more necessary in walking carefully?

The days in which we are living are evil, though not in precisely the same sense as those of the first century. Probably the Christians who first read this letter were chiefly concerned with difficulties arising from having to live in a pagan city where 'uncircumspect' conduct might bring disaster on the whole Church, while we are over-shadowed by evils affecting the whole of the civilized world. But though the evils with which we have to grapple are on a larger scale, the Apostle's advice is no less applic-able now than when he gave it. We, too, have to do what we can to redeem the time, and we, too, shall fail unless we look carefully around and estimate the situation in its stark reality. We shall do no good by shutting our eyes and hoping for the best.

There are various opinions on what Christians ought to do in these evil days and this is not the place for controversy on the subject, but I venture to think there can be no real dispute that we need both the intellectual and emotional virtues in approaching our problems. Never may we cease to feel compassion or to love mercy and peace, but neither may we forget the claim of justice and truth. The two kinds of virtue are not necessarily at odds. Justice and peace may 'kiss each other' and in fact we may well believe that peace gained at the price of justice cannot endure, nor can mercy unguided by knowledge and reflection be effective. 'Understanding what the will of the Lord is', writes St Paul. That Lord is loving wisdom and merciful justice.

Twenty-first Sunday after Trinity

THE QUIET MIND

Quietness is a scarce commodity in our civilization, and many of us find that to purchase it is beyond our means. Though less expensive, quietness of mind is no less difficult to secure, so that, in addition to the din of cars, planes and other assailants of peace, we have to endure the mental disquiet of the political and social unrest of a world in rapid change.

Yet one of the aims and rewards of the life of the Spirit is that 'quiet mind' for which today's Collect teaches us to pray. In this it agrees with the New Testament. In what is perhaps the first Christian letter ever written by St Paul he urges his readers to 'be ambitious' for another gift of the Spirit beyond the zeal and active charity which they have shown; let them strive for quietness of mind, which will enable them to look after their own business without distraction (1 Thessalonians 4:11.)

The quiet mind cannot be achieved by a policy of shutting one's eyes to facts. A man who refuses to take notice of the troubles of the world in which he lives is not only withdrawing his help when it is needed, he is trying to set up a private fools' paradise. He cannot really contract out of the responsibilities of his membership of a nation and of the human race. The quiet mind must be the outcome of victory over anxieties not of running away from them.

The Collect, still in harmony with the New Testament, links quietness of mind with 'pardon and peace' and 'being

cleansed from all our sins'; that is, it associates the calming
of the mind with the solution of an inner conflict. But the
conflict has not been won by the mind of the man. It has
been won by God, and through faith in Him. The divided
mind has handed its problem over to God and has committed itself to Him as the loving Father who is both willing
and able to pardon and cleanse. Reconciliation with God is,
for the Christian believer, the core and essence of a mind at
peace.

This quietness of mind is the opposite of the fools'
paradise. It is not terrified into stagnation, but active and
alert. And in its quietness is its strength. Anchored on the
inward peace of the Spirit, such a man will not dither in
the face of emergency or despair at disaster, for his trust is
not in luck, or chance, or in some future turn of events—
it is in the Eternal.

This restless age needs to acquire quietness of mind if it
hopes to escape catastrophe, and its physical restlessness
may be partly a symptom of its mental and spiritual
rootlessness. Who knows whether those who speed so
senselessly from place to place may not be looking un-
consciously for somewhere where there is peace—and not
finding it.

Twenty-second Sunday after Trinity

HOLY FRIENDSHIP

'I thank my God whenever I think of you': so St Paul begins his letter to his friends in Philippi (Philippians 1:3). Was there ever a loftier expression of friendship? The ancients, and particularly Aristotle, thought highly of friendship as a part of the good life, but I think none of them ever said anything like this. To St Paul friendship was holy, a gift of grace to be received with thanksgiving. If we pray at all, no doubt we pray for our friends when they are in trouble, but how often do we thank God for them?

If we did so more frequently we should get to know them better, for we should be led to ask ourselves why we have reason to be thankful. It may be that we should find that not everything in them is praiseworthy, but if our friendship is real we shall not criticize or break away, we shall see more clearly what to pray for and how to help. We are thinking of true friendship, which is always based on some good and is never purely selfish. In this it differs from those spurious associations which usurp the title and are, in fact, only alliances for profit, for pleasures, or even conspiracies. True and lasting friendships are knit together most often by the sharing in common of admiration or enthusiasm for some value such as beauty in art or music, or for some cause which unites the friends in effort and hope.

St Paul was well aware of this, for he goes on to say that his prayers for the Philippians were always joyful because they were engaged with him in the common cause of Christ; when he lay in prison they were with him in sympathy and hope, and he was sure that they would continue in the path on which they had begun. And so his prayer for them is simply that they will develop further: that their love might grow richer, not more fervent or sincere, but more mature. The root of the matter was in them and he earnestly desired that, through increasing knowledge and insight, their love would be discriminating, that they would learn by experience the real values of life.

It is not to be recommended that we should become introspective about our friendships. To be always analysing our relation with our friends leads to self-consciousness, which kills spontaneity. We must be natural and free in our speech with them, and it is best that any influence which we have on them should be unconscious and undesigned. But it is right that we should keep our friendships in repair and in good order, asking ourselves from time to time whether they are gifts of grace for which both our friends and we have reason to be thankful. And if we conclude that they fall short of the ideal which St Paul exemplifies, we shall be well advised if we do not start by trying to change our friend but postpone that until we have carefully researched on possible defects in ourselves.

Twenty-third Sunday after Trinity

CAESAR'S RIGHTS

'Render unto Caesar the things that are Caesar's': these words of Jesus which occur in today's Gospel (Matthew 22) are not a clever evasion of an awkward question; they are always with us. How far ought a Christian to conform to, and support, the civilization and secular order in which he lives?

Jesus repudiates the idea that there is no obligation. Caesar has at least the right to levy taxes to maintain law and order, but he adds—'unto God the things that are God's'. There is an obligation which transcends that of earthly citizenship.

The principle which Jesus here enunciated was adopted and developed by the Apostles. They insisted on respect for the government and its officials as doing a necessary work and, in this sense, ordained by God. They insisted no less on the limits of obedience. It happens that the Epistle (Philippians 3:17–21) contains a phrase of St Paul's, thrown out, as it were, in passing, which illuminates the overriding obligation to God. Rebuking some most unsatisfactory Christians, he says, 'Our citizenship is in heaven.' The unworthy believers were not outraging the law, they were all right with Caesar, but they were offending against the city of God, exiling themselves from it.

The New Testament teaching about heaven differs from some other doctrines of eternal life by being the opposite of individualist. The gift of eternal life does not confer on us a select and solitary blessedness, or a private and exclusive vision of God; it is not a 'flight of the alone to the Alone'; it is a communion and fellowship in Christ, which has its own principles and laws.

The Christian, therefore, has two duties. He has to do his best to convert Caesar, which means in modern terms to seek to bring the earthly society, its laws and customs and its purposes and ideals into harmony with those of the heavenly city; he must labour to permeate the life of city and nation with the spirit of Christ. But also he must 'keep himself unspotted from the world'; in other words, he must not sink into a placid conformity with the *mores* of his environment. We must beware lest Caesar should convert us.

Perhaps we are too contented and too much at home in the world. Another Apostolic light on the problem is that the Christian must feel an alien, a stranger and pilgrim— and so he often will, if his citizenship is really in heaven.

Twenty-fourth Sunday after Trinity

CHRISTIAN FRIENDSHIP

A criticism sometimes made of Christian ethics is that friendship is less valued in its idea of the good life than in some pagan moralists or than in the Old Testament. One evidence for this opinion is the alleged absence of devoted friendships from the New Testament. There is nothing, for example, corresponding to the moving stories of David and Jonathan and of Ruth and Naomi.

The Christian elevation of *agape* to the supreme value modifies the conception of friendship. The close friendships of non-Christian moral stories have an undertone of exclusiveness which is hard to reconcile with the principle of love for all neighbours.

Yet the second lesson at Mattins tomorrow (the Epistle to Philemon) is a precious first-hand record of friendship in the Christian community of the first century. It should be read in the New English Bible, which rightly sacrifices the exact translation of the Greek words to give the real meaning and spirit of the one private letter from St Paul which has come down to us. In the obscurity which prevails over most of the daily lives of primitive Christians one little patch is vividly illuminated. The spotlight discloses a group of friends.

The Apostle, in prison, writes to his friend Philemon about a runaway slave who has been converted and is being sent back to his master with the letter. Onesimus, the bearer of the letter, has engaged the affection of St Paul so that he speaks of him as a 'son'. It is evident that St Paul hopes Philemon will give Onesimus his liberty. The Apostle, though in prison, is sufficiently hopeful of regaining his own liberty to ask his friend to keep a room for him.

We do not know whether Philemon did as St Paul asked, but it is reasonable to suppose that he did, because he evidently kept the letter, and we may hope that the stories in the early Church that the slave Onesimus became a prominent bishop are true. We have no clue to the place where St Paul was imprisoned, and consequently we have no data on which we could base any conjecture whether Paul ever occupied the guest-room for which he asked. Perhaps the fact that Philemon must have carefully preserved the letter suggests that it was the last that came from his revered friend before his martyrdom.

But these things are interesting details compared with the outstanding disclosure of the kind of people the Christians were. Philemon's family circle was only one among many of friends united in common loyalty, service, and hope who called themselves 'brothers' and 'sisters' in Christ. Barriers fell before Him, and men and women who would have had nothing in common until they knew Him were united in love.

CELESTIAL FRIEND

Early in the present century someone (was it William James?) coined the phrase, 'a friend behind phenomena', to describe what belief in God meant to him. I suppose in many religions the idea of a friendly deity has a place and indeed in some the purpose of sacrifice is to change hostile powers into kindly ones. Where polytheism prevails no logical difficulty arises; where there are many gods one or more may be credited with benevolent intentions in contrast with others of the opposite disposition. In the case of the great monotheistic religions, Judaism, Christianity, and Islam, however, the conception of the Deity as a friend is not so easy; it may even sound blasphemous in ears accustomed to praises of transcendent Godhead. How can the High and Holy One who inhabits eternity, He who dwells in light unapproachable, the everlasting creative Mind be truly represented as like a human friend who sympathizes with our daily concerns and passing anxieties? We must own that some ways of thinking and speaking about God by simple-minded Christians, if adopted by better-informed believers, would verge upon irreverence. And yet the human need for a divine friend and companion remains even in the most sophisticated. Religion does not subsist only on abstract immensities, nor is the religious experience unmixed fear and trembling. Though we may agree that to think of God as a magnified man is a dangerous error, to think of

Him as only transcendent and inhuman is even worse.

Religion is about individual human lives, with their suffering, temptations, terrors and their joy and laughter. Homely and serviceable religion demands that we should be free to bring to God the things that would interest our nearest and dearest friend, and moreover that we should believe He cares and can help. It is good to know that God knows all the stars and all the material universe, that He understands all the processes of nature, but in my need it seems better still that he knows my pains, my apprehensions, my anxieties, everything about me and that, like a true friend, He will never forsake or forget me, so that if the whole human race rejected me and wiped out all memory of me, I should still be known and loved by God. The Christian when he thinks of God as his eternal friend has authority for his belief in the New Testament. In the Gospel of John, which presents the Lord Jesus as the Incarnate Word of God, we read that He called His disciples not servants but friends and said that those who had seen Him had seen the Father. One cannot help asking whether Christianity can still be called monotheistic when it believes in so many different divine activities: Creator, Eternal Mind, Judge, Saviour, and Friend.

SAINTS' DAYS
AND OTHER OCCASIONS

UNITY OCTAVE

During the week when Christians are praying for unity among themselves it is fitting that we should think of unity in service as well as in worship for worship is imperfect and unreal unless it evokes the desire to serve.

The test which Jesus laid down for His disciples who worshipped 'in spirit and in truth' was not fervency of feeling or even growth in religious knowledge; it was 'by their fruits ye shall know them'.

We may perhaps think that the theologians who have been concerned, rightly, in defining orthodox belief have often been unduly negligent of this word of their Master's. What a different story we should have to tell of the history of the Church if the problems of division and reunion had always been approached first with the question, What are the fruits? and only secondly with the question, What are the doctrines?

One of the hopeful signs of the times is the growth of co-operation in Christian service. It is alleged that there is less voluntary service to works of love now than there used to be, and it seems in fact that the number of persons of leisure who can give anything like their whole time has diminished, but the amount of gratuitous and skilled work for such organizations as the Marriage Guidance Council is considerable, and probably the quality of the service is higher than it has ever been before.

In this kind of activity Christian unity is being born.

Those who engage in it do not ask to what denomination their colleagues belong, or even if they have any Church allegiance, but it is a fact of which all are aware that most of them are there because Christ has sent them; their service is the expression of their worship.

When we work for the common cause of Christian living and Christian home-life along with men and women whose church loyalties are not ours, but who are evidently striving for the same end and with the same motive as ourselves, we know that there is already a unity of all those who love the Lord Jesus Christ.

There is a kind of service which is not sufficiently recognized—that of thinking. Great questions exist, many of them of practical importance, on which the Christian conscience needs enlightenment. We can all name off-hand several of them. The way to world peace and the duty of Christians with regard to it are the most obvious, but there are many others. For example the whole field of sexual behaviour bristles with problems to which some Christian answer must be sought. It is not the Christian way to leave these to the experts. The whole Church is called to assist in the task.

In our worship we pray for light, for the enlightenment of our minds, and if we are sincere in our petitions, we must mean that we should have power to exercise them effectively and to make some contribution to the under-standing of that 'pure and peaceable wisdom' which comes from God.

Thought without prayer and prayer without thought are both likely to be sterile, but thought and prayer together are the true and reasonable service of God.

25 January

CONVERSION OF ST PAUL

The Conversion of St Paul was on any view, an important historical event. We cannot imagine the New Testament without his writings, nor what Christianity would have been if he had never been enlisted in its service. From the human point of view, the conversion was a highly improbable event, and even when it had happened the chances against St Paul becoming a leader were formidable. Naturally enough, the change from persecutor to Apostle so quickly effected was suspect and there are indications in the New Testament that the courage and generosity of men like Barnabas had to encounter criticism.

Paul, to a hostile observer, might well have appeared a trouble-maker. He did not seem to be open to reasonable compromise for the sake of peace. In his letter to the Galatians he dwells, with a certain satisfaction, on the fact that at Antioch he had severely rebuked St Peter for unprincipled conduct. To the end of his life there were many Christians who doubted very seriously whether the conversion of St Paul had been a boon or a disaster. And something of the kind may be noticed throughout the history of the Church. His teaching had been found difficult, or disturbing, and has been either explained away or forgotten and today we have scholars in the Church who think that St Paul is the real creator of 'Christianity', introducing into the company of the followers of the Messiah Jesus beliefs which had no place in the original message.

Yet, in spite of all that can be said on the other side, we recognize that the Conversion of St Paul must remain as one of the decisive events in the history of Christianity and that we simply could not do without his letters in our Bible. Without them we should be at a loss how to express the gospel in which we believe and we should not have the clear proclamation of the nature of the Church as the Body of Christ and of the need that it should be at unity in itself.

When we are praying for Christian unity we ought never to forget St Paul, for two reasons; first, because he dwells so forcibly on the unity of the Spirit, and secondly, because he shows, by his example, that unprincipled compromise is not the way towards unity in the truth. We should be glad that neither love of peace nor deference hindered St Paul from 'opposing St Peter to his face' when the reality of Christian fellowship was at stake.

2 February

THE PURIFICATION

St Luke in his Gospel seems to attach importance to the utterances of the old prophet Simeon on the occasion when the infant Jesus was 'Presented' in the Temple, as the Prayer Book calls it. I think he felt that they prepared readers for the narrative which followed by indicating the circumstances of Christ's mission (Luke 2:29–35). Simeon predicts the 'falling and rising' of individuals as a result of Christ's work, the abusive reaction against it, the piercing of Mary's heart and as a consequence, the disclosure of the thoughts of many hearts. The suggestion is of anxiety, conflict and dangerous thoughts which man dared not utter. The impact of Christ and His message would startle many into realistic thinking and frank speech. We too are living when crisis looms but its shape is unclear so that we often think it may be safer to keep our ideas to ourselves. When Jesus was born crisis was imminent, so to speak, 'in church and state' as it is today. We cannot turn away from the distracted 'world' to the secure and peaceful Church. Wherever we look for our earthly spiritual home we shall find men are engaged in 'interior dialogue' on their faith. Have we any guidance in the New Testament for such a situation?

One negative precept seems to emerge: don't bottle your thoughts up. Enlarge the dialogue by including others who can understand your perplexity; try to make some contribution to 'the mind of the church'. Though negative in form this precept can have positive effects. Now the movement towards Christian unity, which we all admit in principle is in harmony with the mind of Christ, is taking form. There are two attitudes which can be adopted by rational believers after honest thought—either for or against. The one attitude which cannot be justified is that of indifference and refusal to consider the question. And yet if the movement is checked it will be because of the number of believers who 'don't know' because they have never really tried.

5 April

ST MARK

For the Christian there is an indissoluble connexion between goodness and holiness. It has not always been so, and originally the term 'holy' had no ethical implication.

We owe the insight that there can be no true holiness without righteousness largely to the Hebrew prophets.

Today we are apt to identify goodness with religion and even to think that the value of religion consists of inculcating a sense of duty and responsibility. A child may say 'religion makes us good', and no less an authority than Immanuel Kant seems to have had much the same idea. Public worship, he thought, was to be encouraged because it served to remind people of the moral law and of the reverence due to it.

Both the child and Kant are, of course, right up to a point, but they give a very limited view of religion. Holiness and goodness, though closely related, are not identical.

We can probably think of some persons who are plainly good, but to whom we should not naturally apply the term 'holy', and it may be that we know some who could be called holy, but who are not particularly 'good' in any accepted sense of the word.

It is not altogether easy to define where the distinction lies because we never come across either quality, so to speak, in an undiluted form. In our experience we do not find men who are good but have no tinge of holiness, or men who are holy but who have no moral virtue.

159

It seems that the typically 'good' man is one who has adopted for himself a high standard of conduct, is guided by unselfish ideals and sets his will resolutely to keep the standard and be true to the ideals. The respect that we have for such a man is due to the fact that we understand, at least in part, the effort and perseverance which such consistency entails. We feel we could not do that; or at least we have not done it.

To some it may appear a defect in the New Testament that it has nothing to say about such persons. It would hardly be an exaggeration to suggest that it does not even recognize their existence. The master word in this connexion, if we follow the guidance of the Bible, is not goodness but holiness, 'without which no man shall see the Lord'.

In the Gospel for St Mark's Day (John 15:1–11) we are presented with one of the great symbols by which the Christian conception of holiness is set forth. 'I am the vine, ye are the branches; he that abideth in me and I in him, the same beareth much fruit.'

Holiness, wholeness, good conduct and noble deeds are not to be thought of as products of the unaided human will. The good character does not have to be built up by long continued effort. It is there, waiting for us to claim it.

I do not have to strain to be my 'best self', whatever that may be. My goodness consists in 'putting on Christ', being 'in Him', recognizing that I am 'a branch' of the true vine—the idea is expressed in many forms. The act of will is simplified until it becomes concentrated on one point—the determination to abide in Him.

That is the root of the psychological difference between

the holy and the good. The moral hero never relaxes, driving himself on his chosen course; the holy man can leave the matter to God, so long as he does not cut the communication with the Source of his life. He does not think of himself as 'good' or pride himself on his virtue, for he knows that, left to himself, he would cease to be. 'Why callest thou me good? One is good, even God.'

1 May

Few utterances are more futile than vague and general exhortations not to be anxious. The victim of this affliction knows well enough that it confuses his mind and weakens his will, and to tell him so only adds to his distress.

Cheery reminders that 'it may not happen' are of little effect, for his anxiety arises from the uncertainty of the future, and 'it may not' implies that it may. An unfounded optimism is not the cure: there can be none which does not face the situation, admitting all the possibilities.

We may have more respect for those who, with Stoic pride steel themselves against all vicissitudes and disasters resolute to endure without whimpering. But we may well doubt whether our will is capable of such unswerving steadfastness and in such noble pride we may see little hope or joy.

When Jesus exhorts us not to be anxious about our lives He is not vague.

He is addressing those who have chosen to serve God rather than 'Mammon' so definitely that they 'hold to one and despise the other' and He asks them to consider who He is that they serve. They depend upon the loving will of the heavenly Father who knows all their needs.

We find an extension of this thought in the Gospel for today where Jesus says to His disciples, 'Let not your heart be troubled; ye believe in God, believe also in me. In my Father's house are many mansions.' (John 14:1.) The remedy for anxiety which Jesus proffers is faith in God and in His love for all who turn to Him.

It will be said, all this is well enough and no doubt anyone who is completely certain that God is love and cares for him need never be harassed by anxiety, for he will be sure that in the end all things will be well, but the real difficulty lies in this—how to hold fast to this faith when so many aspects of the world and so much of our experience seem to contradict it. Who could deny the force of this objection? There are times when circumstances overwhelm us and we almost lose our hold upon our faith. Just when we most desperately need it, it begins to fail.

But why should we expect that our faith should be firm in dark days if we did not cultivate it when they were bright? If we have left it at the back of our minds, as something there but not attended to except in emergency, we ought not to be surprised that it loses power. While the prospect is fair we may build up our faith in God by living consciously in His presence, preparing for the storms that may come to shake it.

'Be not anxious about to-morrow', says Jesus. He does not mean that we should not plan for the future. He has no commendation for the imprudent. He means that we should not become emotionally involved in what has not yet happened and may never happen.

We live today and need all our faith and energy for that; sufficient for the day is its evil. When we have overcome that evil with good we shall be prepared to meet tomorrow.

11 June

❖◇◇◇◇◇◇◇◇◇◇◇◇◇◇◇◇✳◇◇◇◇◇◇◇◇◇◇◇◇◇◇◇◇❖

ST BARNABAS

St Barnabas, is one of those New Testament characters of whom we should like to know more, but enough is told to justify his apostolic name which means 'son of exhortation', or of 'consolation'. As the Collect for the day asserts, he was evidently 'endued with singular gifts of the Holy Ghost'. A phrase in the 'Epistle' (Acts 21:23) illustrates one of them—when he came to Antioch 'and had seen the grace of God he was glad'. An innovation had occurred which caused anxiety to some Christians; the Gospel had been preached with effect to Greeks, that is to pagans who had no background of Jewish belief or practice. Barnabas, sent to investigate the matter, recognized the work of the Holy Spirit in this new enterprise and rejoiced. This recognition and gladness had historical importance.

This incident suggests that gladness can be a good guide to a man's real character. I have heard it said that one can judge a man by what he laughs at, but this is probably too superficial a sign, for laughter is often a sudden reaction to the incongruous and little more, but gladness and joy go deeper and reveal the man. If I know what evokes a lifting of the heart, what makes the world seem brighter to anyone, including myself, I have an insight into the springs of personal life.

The New Testament has not passed over this matter in silence. Joy is the second fruit of the Spirit, after love, in

164

St Paul's list, and in describing the ideal of the Christian life he reiterates the call to 'rejoice in the Lord always'. Was he thinking of his friend Barnabas, who had been glad at Antioch, when he wrote these words?

Nor is the dark side of the picture omitted. St Paul contrasts the joy of those who are inspired by divine charity with those who 'rejoice in iniquity'. And this also is a possibility in human experience. When we read descriptions of the Jewish concentration camps in Hitler's Germany we recoil with horror at the wholesale massacres, but perhaps the most challenging aspect is the glimpse that we have of the men who took part in the methodical slaughter. Can it be that human beings laughed and rejoiced at the torture of children? It has been and it can be.

Not all who rejoice in iniquity are monsters. There are some whose vices are more attractive and respectable, being connected with the natural lusts of the flesh and avarice, but they are not content to keep their evil ways to themselves, they are glad when they can initiate others into their ways.

The Christian has joy and gladness, we are told, and we are to find occasion for them where we recognize the grace of God. It may be that we narrow our search too much and fail to notice many things that should make our day brighter. Probably Barnabas did not expect to meet joy in Antioch—only a tiresome dispute—but, being the man he was he encountered gladness. If we 'walked in the Spirit' more consistently our eyes would be opened to see His work in the faith and love of many quite ordinary persons, and we should be glad.

24 June

ST JOHN THE BAPTIST

The figure of John the Baptist stands out clearly in the Gospels. We have a coherent picture of the character and mission of the forerunner of Christ, but it is not altogether easy to construct an idea of his beliefs about Christ.

St John's Gospel would suggest that from the beginning he recognized Jesus as the Messiah, 'He who should come', but in Matthew we find him sending two disciples to ask this very question, 'Art thou he that should come, or do we look for another?'

Perhaps the Baptist, in prison and near to death, had begun to question his earlier conviction. The situation in which he found himself seemed to mark the end of his own ministry, and what he heard of the activities of Jesus did not appear to be the bringing in of the Kingdom of God as he had imagined it.

We do not know whether the answer Jesus gave reassured John. It was short, almost abrupt. The messengers were told to report the things that they had heard and seen —the works of healing power and the Gospel proclaimed to the poor.

Jesus did not offer theological argument but evidential facts. By His fruits He would be known.

We may sympathize with the Baptist. In his days of affliction and defeat he was haunted by the doubt whether his hope and faith, on which he had built his career of self-sacrifice, might be after all an illusion. He craved for a definite answer, yes or no.

In our smaller sphere we, too, may have known the same experience. When we needed it most our faith was weakened.

In times of prosperity our belief in the love of God and in the Good Shepherd who cares for each one of His flock was firm and bright, but when trouble comes and we are perplexed by life's problems where is our trust in Christ?

At such times it is little use to go over again all the arguments and reasons which have supported and clarified our faith in the past. The debate can be endless, and we have no time to wait for its conclusion. We need our faith now.

The method which Jesus employed in dealing with John is valid for us. The change in my circumstances from gladness to sorrow has not altered the situation in general. When I made a decision to be a member of Christ and to adhere to God I was moved by the power of God in Christ to do works of love in and through human creatures. Let me remember that and the days when I knew in myself the grace of God.

Faith is never simply an intellectual belief or an emotional response; there is always an act of choice, a movement of the will, a decision. There is a point where the believer has ceased to regard the question, 'Art thou he that should come?' as open and has committed himself to the answer, 'Yes.'

Thenceforth, though he does not cease to think or to be disturbed by difficulties, he holds fast to his foundation truth. The tree of the life of the spirit will never grow if we are always digging up its roots.

~~~~~~~~~~~~~~~~~~❋~~~~~~~~~~~~~~~~~~

ST PETER

'Public Relations' is, I suppose, a term which has a modern ring, but what it stands for is ancient enough. Indeed St Peter writes about it as a problem for the Church of his day, and an urgent one (1 Peter 2).

We can easily understand why it should be so. The Church was a minority movement which practised a worship strange to the majority; it was a close-knit fellowship with its own rules of conduct and it regarded itself as a 'holy people' separate from the world.

Resentments and suspicions are soon aroused by such communities, and when St Peter wrote this letter they were becoming dangerous. Not long afterwards Nero was able to utilize them to divert the anger of the citizens of Rome from himself to the calumniated Christians.

It is instructive to observe how the Christian deals with the question. First, he recognizes the root of the trouble. It lies in the inevitable situation of the Church. Those who form its members are 'strangers and pilgrims' in the world. Though they are in it, they are not of it, and their faith and hope are fixed on God and His Kingdom. There can, therefore, be no thought of any radical compromise or accommodation to the standards and ideals of the society in which their pilgrimage was set.

Reading between the lines we may suspect that some Christians were inclined to meet anger with anger, and contempt with contempt. That is not the Apostle's way.

The false accusations are to be met and refuted by the patient example of the Christian fellowship—'having your behaviour seemly among the Gentiles'.

The Greeks expressed their idea of goodness in two words and not, as we do, in one. They may be roughly translated as 'good' and 'beautiful', and St Peter here uses the words which indicates the beauty, attractiveness, or seemliness of a virtuous life.

He means that the holiness of the Christian fellowship should be not only an inner, spiritual condition but plainly manifested to critical observers. He is, after all, only repeating the words of Jesus, 'Let your light so shine before men that they may see your good works and glorify your father.'

The second point which he makes is concerned with the duties of citizenship and would need an essay in itself. We pass over it here to refer to the third piece of advice—that against fanaticism.

The Apostle is evidently concerned to distinguish the gospel from the number of irrational superstitions which were rife.

The Christian is to be ready always to 'give an answer to every man that asketh a reason concerning the hope that is in him, yet with meekness and fear'. Matthew Arnold's word 'the sweet reasonableness of Jesus' is no doubt inadequate, but it is not far from the mark as a description of the attitude of this Epistle.

What could be more impressive than the calm assurance that the gospel is the truth, and, quietly stated by those who have thought about it, will make its way into the minds and consciences of men?

Public relations of the Church are not the same today as they were then. The 'public' is different; and the methods must be different, but surely the basic principles have not changed.

I have heard it said that no advertisement can sell a poor article. I hope that is true, but certainly it is true that the primary need for effective public relations of the Church is that it should be manifestly the Church of Christ—'that wherein ye are spoken against, they may be put to shame who revile your good manner of life in Christ'.

22 July

<><><><><><><><><><><><><><><>✳<><><><><><><><><><><><><><><>

ST MARY MAGDALEN

We may be glad that St Mary Magdalen has been restored to the list of major saints in the revised Anglican calendar and that her festival is now celebrated among those of the Apostles. Without her we should lack an example of a special kind of holiness—that of the passionate penitent. Though the Gospels tell us no more than that Jesus had cast out of her seven devils, the tradition of the Church from early times identified her with 'the woman who was a sinner' who anointed the Lord's feet while He was at dinner and of whom He said, 'Her great love proves that her many sins have been forgiven' (Luke 7:36–50). The image which Christian piety has built up of this woman is probably not far from the truth and is, at any rate, one of which there are many examples. She was, we may suppose, of a passionate and reckless temperament who was capable of throwing prudence and convention to the winds for the sake of what seemed to be love. The wonder on which the imagination of Christians dwelt is that she was called and sanctified by Christ to be a witness of His resurrection.

The conversion of this passionate penitent was of a type that not only philosophers but many staid and sober persons regard as questionable. Apparently it had almost no intellectual content, and was not associated with any logical reflection. It was the outcome of a personal encounter with Jesus, and the holiness which shone in Him evoked in her an overwhelming response. Nor was her temperament changed in her conversion; it was still passionate and reckless. Without thought of convention or propriety she manifested her devotion in uninhibited and extravagant acts.

The Church tends to look askance at enthusiasts such as she and to prefer as its norm the docile and respectable. In these days we have learned a new word to indicate our disapproval of the passionate penitents; we call them 'exhibitionists'. The Magdalen's festival year by year should remind us that Christ had a more liberal conception of holiness and of the potentialities of erring human beings. He did not reject the penitent because she was passionate.

Some, who neither look nor act like the Magdalen, beneath a calm exterior hide a passionate nature which by stern discipline they keep in check, damping down by reason and will the fire within. They deserve respect and sympathy. But perhaps there is another way, or rather a positive strategy which can make the discipline joyful. We may accept our passionate nature and turn it towards a new object. Mary Magdalen found her focus in Christ and poured out her emotional power on the quest for the holiness she had discerned in Him. She still had the impulse to give herself away, she still felt that the world was well lost for love, but it was a divine love and a divine Object that she knew. How right it is that the Epistle for her day begins, 'The love of Christ constraineth us.' (2 Corinthians 5:14).

25 July

ST JAMES

Tomorrow the Church commemorates St James, called 'the Great' to distinguish him from the two other Jameses of the New Testament. Readers of Acts must often wonder what the other apostles were doing while Peter and Paul were so active, and an impression is left on some minds that the majority of the original band faded out.

James is one of whom we hear nothing for about fourteen years; in the life-time of Jesus he was prominent, being the brother of John and one of the four disciples who head the lists in the Gospels. Together with his brother he was called 'son of thunder' by Jesus, and either he or his mother put in a claim that he should, with John, occupy the place of honour next to Jesus himself in the Kingdom of God. We have the outline sketch of a man who had plenty of energy and was capable of forcible expression while not devoid of self-confidence and ambition.

Why this silence? Was he dead or had he abandoned the cause of the gospel? He comes into history again by his public death. The 'son of thunder' had not been silent, and when Herod Agrippa wanted to gain popularity by killing a heretic he chose James, no doubt because his outspoken witness to Christ had made him a recognized leader.

The story of the rise of the Church is not completely known because the main document on which we depend, the Acts of the Apostles, concentrates attention necessarily on the two most prominent missionary leaders, whereas a full understanding would need a whole series of 'acts' covering the lives of many apostolic persons.

The legends which have come down to us are for the most part unreliable and owe more to pious imagination than to memory. About St James we may at least hope the legend is true that the man who had engineered his martyrdom was so moved by James's bearing that he confessed the faith of Christ and shared the fate of his victim, the saint kissing his penitent betrayer at the foot of the scaffold.

To the detached observer the life of James the Great may well seem too short to have much significance. Chosen by the Lord Jesus for leadership and trained by association with Him, just at the time when the crisis became acute he is removed by death. We may be sure that was not how James looked upon his fate. Enough for him that he had been faithful in the testing time and had not faltered in his witness; enough, too, for his comrades in the service of Christ that he had been incorporated into the 'cloud of witnesses' who from heavenly places prayed for those who continued the conflict on earth.

6 August

THE TRANSFIGURATION

When we read the writings of some saintly persons a doubt creeps into our minds. Do not they seem so entirely concentrated on the salvation and sanctification of themselves, and on the holy joy that comes to them in their devotions, that we suspect a spiritual selfishness? We are probably wrong, and their love for others is far stronger than our own, but it is at least possible to be very devout and to have wonderful spiritual experience while sadly neglecting the duty to our neighbours.

The Gospel for the Feast of the Transfiguration of our Lord (Mark 9:2–10), describes an incident which has many implications and more than one interpretation. Some have even thought it is a resurrection appearance of Christ which has somehow become displaced. Whatever else it may be, it is certainly the record of a deeply impressive moment of insight shared by three apostles, in which they perceived something of the true nature of the Man with whom they had tramped the roads of Galilee. It was a moment too when they felt very sure of God and very near to Him— and in His presence was joy as well as fear, an awed delight. What more natural then than St Peter's impulsive cry, 'Master, it is good for us to be here!' and his hope to make the situation permanent by building three tents for Jesus, Moses, and Elijah; but it could not be; the Transfiguration was an interlude in the stern business of the redemption of mankind, and soon the three disciples were following Jesus down the mountain to plunge once more into the world where sorrow and sin abounded. The Transfiguration was not an escape, but a brief refreshment of the spirit.

Is it wrong, then, to love oneself in the spiritual life or to hope for our own salvation and our perfection? In I John 3:2 we are encouraged to seek our fulfilment, or perhaps rather our own transfiguration. 'Now are we sons of God and it doth not yet appear what we shall be, but we know that when He shall appear we shall be like Him, for we shall see Him as He is.'

The man who wrote these words was one who knew very well what transfigured moments mean when the soul rests in the immediate knowledge of God, but he is of all the New Testaments writers the most emphatic in asserting that it is impossible really to love God if we do not love our brothers, and that he who loves his brothers is, whether he knows it or not, loving God.

We dare not hope for a solitary perfection. 'The flight of the alone to the Alone', the phrase of the pagan mystic Plotinus, is not a Christian formula. Our perfection does not lie along this path, but rather along that which leads to the fellowship of 'just men made perfect'.

21 September

ST MATTHEW

On the feast of St Matthew we think with gratitude of the Gospel which bears his name. To it we owe much of our knowledge of the teaching of Jesus, of the Sermon on the Mount, and the way of humility and love. In this Gospel, too, we are told of words which have the harsh tone of revenge. At the end of the trial of Jesus before Pontius Pilate the Roman Governor washed his hands as a symbolic gesture, saying, 'I am clean of the blood of this just man,' to which the people replied 'with one voice'—'His blood be upon us and on our children'. Thereupon, Pilate gave way and gave the victim up to be crucified (Matthew 27:24ff.). If Matthew wrote these words he probably had no idea of the misery they would cause. The Old Testament, after all, has much to say about visiting the sins of the fathers on the children. When Jesus was speaking once about the future of His disciples, he foretold that a time would come when enemies would kill them because they thought that by doing so they were serving God; and so it happened. But it also happened that when Christians became powerful they persecuted Jews and for long periods. They too thought sometimes that they were doing God's will and pointed to these words in Matthew in justification. Did not the people of the Jews accept the responsibility of their children for the death of Christ?

This incident is not recorded in the other Gospels and probably it has no basis in fact; but that is not the point.

Even if the words of the people could be established as precisely accurate and it could be proved that all the people joined in the cry and understood what it meant they would have no validity. They imply an absurdity. What could be more incongruous than to think the Son of Man who gave his life as a ransom would be pleased by revenge? And by what right or power could parents devote their children to the conditions of a covenant which held good from one generation to another? To such depths of cruelty and irrationality superstitious ideas can sink. The Hebrew Prophets Jeremiah and Ezekiel had exposed long before the fallacy of transmitted guilt and deferred revenge.

We may discard altogether perhaps the ideas of inherited guilt and deferred revenge, but is there not some misunderstood truth in these conceptions? We may think that we can get on very well without the idea of inherited responsibility, but closer consideration may lead us to think that to heighten our sense of inherited responsibility is one of our urgent needs.

29 *September*

If the phrase may be permitted, angels are unevenly distributed in the Bible. In some parts of Scripture they are not mentioned while in others they are prominent. A striking instance can be noticed in the writings traditionally ascribed to St John. His Gospel omits most references to angels and his letters have no mention of them, but the Revelation of St John, his Apocalypse, is crowded with celestial beings. It is not impossible that he wrote the Apocalypse, but if he did, we must allow that his mind was moving in a different range of images from that in which he wrote his Gospel and letters.

The difference arises from a difference in the conception of God. Angels are conceived as the messengers and soldiers of the Heavenly King. Like an earthly monarch, He has His servants and attendants to do His will and administer His realm. The underlying picture of God is that of the transcendent ruler of the universe. In the Gospel of St John, we read that God is Spirit and is to be worshipped in spirit and in truth. This is a more profound conception of the nature of God. St John most certainly believed that God is transcendent, unapproachable, far beyond man's comprehension, but he also believed that this transcendent God is present in and with the finite spirits of man—the creative Reason immanent in the world.

It is not really possible to reconcile these two conceptions of God except by subordinating one to the other; and I suppose we shall all agree that the Gospel of St John comes nearer to the truth than his Apocalypse. If we have to choose between them, we must hold fast to the belief that God is Spirit. But we do not have to reject the picture of the King of the Universe and His angels altogether. There is no difficulty in believing that there are finite intelligences, invisible to us, who exist in another and higher plane of being. No one would now maintain that the space and time system in which we exist is the only one there can be. And if there are intelligences in other systems which interpenetrate ours, we are at liberty to hope that some of them are serving God and helping us according to His will.

Yet it may be disconcerting at first to recognize that, in the New Testament itself, there are at least two divergent ways of thinking about God. Professor Arnold Toynbee is fond of quoting a sentence from a devout pagan which claims that there must be 'many roads by which men may approach so great a mystery' as the being of God. The New Testament does not say that. Jesus Christ is the Way—on that every writer in the New Testament agrees. The more simple who walk along that way may imagine God as the Great King, and the more thoughtful think of Him as Eternal Spirit, but both may know Him as Father and as Love.

18 October

ST LUKE

A small boy faced by an examination question, What do you know about St Paul? summed up his impressions by writing: 'He was a restless man always moving around from one place to another, and wherever he was he said a few words.'

A superficial view, perhaps, but one which we should bear in mind when we consider the problem of communication as the Early Church saw it. For certainly there was a problem, and it is not altogether clear how the relatively rapid spread of Christianity in the first century was brought about.

For example, we do not know how the Church began in two great centres of the Ancient World, Rome and Alexandria. With our almost excessive apparatus of communication, as we sometimes think, we can hardly imagine the conditions in which a minority movement at that time had to propagate itself.

There were no means of public announcement available, and the only occasions on which publicity was easy, were when someone stirred up a riot. Yet the Gospel spread with amazing celerity.

Of course St Paul was not the only 'restless man'; there must have been many other itinerant evangelists.

The Acts of the Apostles concentrates attention on St Peter and St Paul, and we are apt to forget the other Apostles, who cannot surely have been idle.

And there were others, it seems, for 'evangelists' are mentioned in the Epistle. But probably an even more important factor in the solution of the problem of communication was the work of men and women who had no official status in the Church.

Christians who travelled in their occupations as traders, merchants or slaves did not keep silence about their faith and hope in Christ. Every believer was a missionary. Thus we may say that the first leap forward, and the decisive one, which Christianity made was largely the work of persons who are anonymous.

The problem of communication in those days was solved by personal contacts. Oratory and eloquence played a very little part. St Paul himself, who obviously could speak powerfully if the need arose, is as contemptuous of rhetoric as Plato, though for different reasons, and disclaims all resort to the persuasive arts of 'man's wisdom'.

In personal contacts the attraction of the new way of life was taught and caught by those who were seeking for a more satisfying mode of living than they had known. They found it in those who believed that they were daily in personal contact with Christ.

The problem of communication is urgent in Christianity today. It is not precisely the same problem as that which the Church had to deal with in the first century, and, in some respects, indeed, is radically different, but it may be that part of the answer is the same today as it was then—personal contact and every believer a missionary.

We may at least learn to ask the right questions by reflecting on the creative period of the history of religion: what are we trying to communicate and who are the communicators?

1 November

All Saints' Day offers food for thought in the shape of questions. Most obvious is that posed by the list of canonized saints, which includes some very odd persons, but a more profitable one is the meaning of sainthood. Are we justified in saying that the word signifies a very good man? John Stuart Mill has been called the 'saint of rationalism', I suppose because he was a high-minded and public-spirited person. I think it is a mistake to blur real distinctions by confusing words, and surely there is a real distinction even though we may find it hard to define. That there is a distinction between 'good men' and 'saints' will, I think, be admitted by everyone who asks himself whether all the good men he knows are saints, and perhaps also whether the saints he has heard of are good men in any ordinary sense of the word.

The example of J. S. Mill is instructive. Though no Philistine and appreciative of Wordsworth's poetry his intellect rejected the supernatural as a thing to be reckoned with; he had no positive belief in God, and his ethical theory was Utilitarianism, that is, it identified the good with the useful; useful in social life as promoting the greatest good of the greatest number.

By the light of this theory Mill and many others who accepted it did promote human well-being and deserve our gratitude and admiration as 'good men': useful men. What then is lacking in them that they should not be called 'saints'?

If one wanted to be paradoxical one might say that they did not have a kind of self-regarding quality. Saints have always been concerned about their souls. They have been conscious that they had souls to 'make', to develop that is, their personalities, so that they grew into things of beauty and preciousness in themselves, whether or not in the estimation of society they were useful. The saints of the Christian tradition, and not a few of other traditions, have admitted indeed that in their own power they cannot make their souls beautiful; only the grace of God can do that, but they have prayed for that grace and thrown themselves open to it.

I do not think this implies that all saints must have orthodox beliefs about God, or even that they must believe that a personal God does exist. Spinoza could, with real justification, be called 'the saint of rationalism'. He was a rationalist in a deeper sense than Mill, and his 'intellectual love of God' was a spiritual exercise in which the human spirit, as it were, learned to spread its wings. We, says St Paul, are called to be saints. That means to be useful persons in the community, and also that we should remember that we have a soul to make, so that, even if we were complete failures in usefulness to others, we might still be part of God's lovely treasure.

2 November

Christians have differed on the question whether it is lawful to pray for the dead, but even those who hold most firmly that intercession for them is wrong do not forget their friends who have gone from this world; they remember and commemorate the departed; and when they do this with faith in God, committing themselves and their friends to Him, is not that to pray? Some who have no scruple about prayer for the dead are not content, however, with the form of prayer customary in the Church. The collects refer exclusively to the 'faithful departed' and in this fall short of what our hearts desire. The 'faithful' we think are safe; they have fought the good fight and are at peace. We do not fear for them. But we have known and loved some perhaps who were not, so far as their words and actions indicate, faithful Christians; they did not profess any belief or, if they did, we cannot satisfy ourselves that it affected their lives. One would think that the 'unfaithful departed' needed our prayer most of all.

May we pray for them? This is no academic question for theologians to argue on; for many loving hearts it is of the greatest moment; to a mother, for example, whose son or daughter died to all appearance in a state of sin. She will pray for the child whatever the theologians say, but can she pray in hope, believing that her prayer is in accordance with the mind of Christ?

We must beware of assuming that we know who is

'faithful' and who is not: a steady look at ourselves is likely to suggest that, for most of us, faithfulness is a matter of degree, or of phases. We have not been wholly abandoned to evil, nor have we been consistently indifferent to the needs of others or the obligations of justice and charity; but there have been times when we have lapsed in all these respects. If we were to die tonight we should depart hence as mixed beings, partly faithful and partly unfaithful. We know that we need the mercy and forgiveness of God. Of any sane human being it seems probably true that he is neither faithful nor unfaithful without qualification. The most devoted saint or moral hero bears some imperfection or some lack of sympathy and understanding and, on the other hand, the most inveterate sinner has some seed of virtue in him which could spring up in conditions different from those of his present existence.

In the prophet Ezekiel we read that God says, 'All souls are mine'. In this context the purpose of the saying is to declare that God's judgement is over all human beings, and that is a part of our Christian faith; but it is not the whole truth. We believe that God is not only justice but love. All souls are embraced in the divine Charity. When we commend the soul of a departed friend—or enemy—to God we are allying ourselves with the redeeming love of the Father of all spirits who is revealed in Christ.

❖◇❖◇❖◇❖◇❖◇❖◇❖◇❖◇❖◇❖◇❀◇❖◇❖◇❖◇❖◇❖◇❖◇❖◇❖◇❖

REMEMBRANCE SUNDAY

When Jesus was at table in the house of Simon the Leper a woman came in and poured some expensive perfume on His head, exciting thereby the indignation of some present at such extravagance (Mark 14). Perhaps she guessed that He was near to death, for Jesus defended her by saying that she had anointed Him for burial and added that wherever the gospel was preached her loving gesture would be told as her memorial. And so it has been. We know nothing else for certain about her, but she has her permanent niche in the immortal story. Immediately after we are told that Judas Iscariot went to the chief priests to betray Jesus. We know hardly anything about Judas except that he was the traitor, but he too has his memorial wherever the gospel is preached. When we think of the life of the Saviour we include the impulsive, loving woman and the vindictive, calculating disciple. Light and dark, good and evil are mingled.

So it should be in our memorial of the two world wars. Some today believe that Remembrance Sunday has outlasted its usefulness and should cease to be observed. They are wrong. We need to be reminded that our freedom and welfare have been made possible by a great sacrifice, and we need to be heartened by recalling year by year that, when Britian was in deadly peril, her sons and daughters saved her. A nation which does not honour its heroes is on the way out. But we dare not remember only the splendour of the story and virtues which were displayed by so many who were equal to the day of testing lest we should nourish in our minds the romantic and glamorous delusion about war. We must remember, too, the dark side—the cruelty, the misery, and the lasting evil results of the wars. Though they were the occasion of wonderful courage and devotion to duty in innumerable individuals, they were gigantic evils, and we may add that the advance of knowledge since the last war, far from alleviating the horrors of war, has vastly increased them. Our memories should not gloze over or minimise the devastation of life, culture and morality which the two wars brought to the world; they should stir us to think hard about the causes of war and the way to remove them.

That war is the greatest of evils is held by some, and they have many arguments to support their view. But I would prefer to say that war is the greatest evil for a nation, save one. A greater evil would be to commit the sin of Judas and betray the ideals and values which raise the nation to a moral and spiritual existence; without them we should be no more than a large commercial undertaking. A nation may have to fight or lose its soul. Through the valour of those whom we commemorate at this season, Britain's soul was not lost. It is our part to preserve it.

27 December

⟡

The classical statement of St John's understanding of the Christian life is contained in 1 John 4. On the surface it is a passage of the utmost simplicity, consisting of a series of short sentences and employing none but familiar words, but its implications are profound and invite unlimited reflection. The key words are 'loving' and 'knowing'. Because love is from God, the Apostle claims, everyone who loves is born of God and knows God. The English word 'love' is an unsatisfactory translation of St John's Greek, because it is too wide, covering states of mind and feeling which are very far from the New Testament sense of 'agape'. Thus some erotic passions which have often been confused with the love of which St John speaks are predominantly selfish, aiming at the possession and domination of the beloved.

The Apostle means by love unselfish generosity, which gives without thought of reward. The love which God gives is displayed in the Incarnation, in which the Only Begotten Son of God gives Himself for the salvation of all men. 'We love because He first loved us'; we should not know how to love if He had not revealed to us how He loves. The way of love to our brethren is, so St John asserts, the way to a knowledge of God. We must distinguish between two kinds of knowing—'knowledge about' and 'knowledge of'. The difference is clear enough in our personal relations, for we may know much about another person, many facts, and yet know very little of what he is in himself; only when we love him, have a concern about him, and sincerely desire his welfare do we begin really to know him as a person. St John's thought is that, in so far as we have the kind of love which God has for us, we know Him; we know Him in loving our fellow men.

There has been some talk lately of 'Christian Agnosticism'. In a sense it might be said that St John is not opposed to the idea, in that he recognizes the limits of our knowledge about God. 'No one has seen God at any time'; even the revelatory visions of inspired prophets have fallen short of clear and direct apprehension of the divine nature, but the agnosticism is not absolute, for 'God himself dwells in us if we love one another'.

In these days, when many questions about religious truths are publicly debated, we may be disturbed and find no sure answers to doubts which arise in our minds. Perhaps the problems are beyond our intellectual scope, or indeed of any human intelligence. We may turn in such a predicament to seek knowledge of God where St John looked for it. It is not beyond our capacities to try to love our brethren more sincerely and generously, and prove in experience that 'everyone who loves is a child of God and knows God'.

28 December

A jarring note is struck in the harmonious idyll of the Birth of Christ by the shocking story of the cold-blooded massacre of young children by order of King Herod (Matthew 2:13–18). It comes as a harsh and brutal echo from another world—the world of human existence. Though we may dislike the story there is no inherent improbability in it. Herod at least acts as we might expect a professional player of the power politics game. He had heard that a child born recently was taken by some to be the Messiah and perhaps the true and coming King, but he had no means of identifying the child except that he was believed to have been born in Bethlehem. All successful tyrants are careful to remove all possible rivals before they grow strong and in the circumstances it was clearly necessary to kill all the children of the right age in the district.

We need not think of this massacre as nationwide and possibly the children killed in Bethlehem were fewer than those killed on Britain's highways this week. All the same, it is a shocking story and illustrates the difference in feeling between the first century in the Roman Empire and the present enlightened age. We do not expose unwanted children, but apart from that are we so superior? It can be argued that in this matter of mass massacre the modern world is worse than the ancient. In our days the complete obliteration of nations, races, and tribes has been attempted and we have coined a word to denote this ideal massacre—

'genocide'. Unfortunately genocide is now quite possible.

Rather quaintly, the Church has canonized the infant victims of Herod's power politics and allotted a day in her calendar for their commemoration. We may enlarge the scope of our commemoration by including with the Holy Innocents all those little children who, year after year, have their lives cut short on the highways of their homeland. Can we be complacent and absolve ourselves of all responsibility? Does not a society which tolerates this death-roll by its callousness and carelessness bear an uncomfortable resemblance to Herod? On Holy Innocents day we can remember our contemporary innocents sacrificed to speed. We cannot ask them to forgive us now. I wonder whether Holy Innocents can pray for us.